TAPPED OUT

MATTHEW POLLY

TAPPED OUT

Rear Naked Chokes, the Octagon, and the Last Emperor

AN ODYSSEY IN
MIXED MARTIAL ARTS

GOTHAM BOOKS

GOTHAM BOOKS
Published by Penguin Group (USA) Inc.
375 Hudson Street, New York, New York 10014, U.S.A.
Penguin Group (Canada), 90 Eglinton Avenue East, Suite 700, Toronto, Ontario M4P 2Y3,
Canada (a division of Pearson Penguin Canada Inc.); Penguin Books Ltd, 80 Strand, London
WC2R 0RL, England; Penguin Ireland, 25 St Stephen's Green, Dublin 2, Ireland (a division
of Penguin Books Ltd); Penguin Group (Australia), 250 Camberwell Road, Camberwell,
Victoria 3124, Australia (a division of Pearson Australia Group Pty Ltd); Penguin Books India
Pvt Ltd, 11 Community Centre, Panchsheel Park, New Delhi—110 017, India; Penguin
Group (NZ), 67 Apollo Drive, Rosedale, Auckland 0632, New Zealand (a division of Pearson
New Zealand Ltd); Penguin Books (South Africa) (Pty) Ltd, 24 Sturdee Avenue, Rosebank,
Johannesburg 2196, South Africa

Penguin Books Ltd, Registered Offices: 80 Strand, London WC2R 0RL, England

Published by Gotham Books, a member of Penguin Group (USA) Inc.

First printing, November 2011

13 12 11   8 7 6 5 4 3 2 1
Copyright © 2011 by Matthew Polly

LIBRARY OF CONGRESS CATALOGING-IN-PUBLICATION DATA
Polly, Matthew.
    Tapped out: rear naked chokes, the octagon, and the last emperor, an odyssey in mixed
martial arts / Matthew Polly.
        p. cm.
    Includes bibliographical references and index.
    ISBN 978-1-592-40599-2 (hardcover : alk. paper)   1. Mixed martial arts.   I. Title.
    GV1102.7.M59P65 2011
    796.815—dc23   2011032698

Printed in the United States of America
Set in Adobe Caslon Pro
Designed by Sabrina Bowers

For my teachers

CONTENTS

tapped out, *adj,* [origins: A *tap* is used to make liquid flow from its source. *Tapped out* means there is nothing left to flow. "This keg is tapped out."] **1**: Out of money; broke, penniless. "Can you grab the check? I'm tapped out." **2**: Tired, exhausted, depleted. "After pulling three all-nighters, I was tapped out." ~ *vi* **1**: To signal submission. Used in grappling and mixed martial arts competitions. "When I tightened the choke hold, my opponent tapped out."

A NOTE ON NAMES

I have used actual names except when a subject requested anonymity. The most notable is my better half.

"I don't want you to write about me," she announced, after I was well into this project.

"When we first met I told you I wrote memoirs," I said. "Which part of that didn't you understand?"

"The writing about me part."

"It won't work without you," I declared. "You make me seem likable."

"Flattery will get you everywhere," she relented. "But you can't use my name."

"What am I supposed to do?"

"You can do what they used to do: the first letter of my name followed by a dash."

"You want me to call you M—? That's a visual nightmare."

"Your problem."

"It's my book."

"Would you prefer to sleep on the couch?"

I try not to argue with her. Not only is she smarter than I, she's also tougher. The only advantages I have are height and reach.

"Yes, dear," I conceded. "How about Em Dash?"

"I prefer just Em."

My Cup Runneth Over

> "Courage is resistance to fear, mastery of fear—
> not absence of fear."
>
> —MARK TWAIN

The morning of my fight, I went to Vegas's biggest mixed martial arts (MMA) equipment store to buy a protective cup. I had been training for four months at Xtreme Couture, the Las Vegas gym founded by Hall of Famer Randy Couture. My coach, Joey Varner, had signed me up for Xtreme Couture's upcoming smoker. (The term comes from the smoke-filled rooms where private clubs held unsanctioned boxing matches in the nineteenth century. Like MMA, boxing used to be illegal in a number of states.) One of the smoker's rules was you had to wear a cup.

It's a dumb rule. Not only are cups uncomfortable, but they don't really work. Whether the illegal knee to the groin reverberates through plastic or lands directly on the nads, it'll drop you just the same. Until someone invents the Airbag Cup, which inflates on impact, they will continue to be relatively useless.

I was comparing brands when Scott, the manager of the store and an occasional coach at Xtreme Couture, came over.

"You're fighting tonight, right?" he asked. "Good luck."

Taking my uncomfortable protective cup with me, I drove over to the gym to meet with Joey for our pre-fight prep. Xtreme Couture was a converted warehouse, located near McCarran Airport. In the lobby, there were offices to the left and a retail store to the right, selling MMA equipment and Xtreme Couture clothing. It was an embarrassment of space—two floors, eleven thousand square feet. It made all the previous gyms I had trained in seem like broom closets. There was a full-size boxing ring and an Octagon cage, a cardio area, and a jiu-jitsu mat as big as half a football field. But my favorite part was the physical therapy center with licensed therapists on staff. Only a millionaire fighter in his forties would think to include a physical therapy center in his gym.

The gym's décor was army camouflage. Randy joined the service at eighteen when he inadvertently knocked up his high school sweetheart. In the army he took up Greco-Roman wrestling, nearly making the Olympic team four times, before he switched at the ripe old age of thirty-four to MMA, almost as a lark, and won the heavyweight belt in his first try. The military motif pervaded Xtreme Couture's brand management. The coaches didn't have titles; they had army rankings. Randy was the major general. The coaches were majors and captains.

I guess that made me the cannon fodder.

As I arrived at Xtreme, Joey started talking excitedly. This was a good sign. The only times Joey was quiet was when he was trying not to lose his temper—as if he were counting to ten in his head. In both looks and personality, Joey reminded me of Special Agent Anthony Dinozzo on the TV show *NCIS*: a constant stream of teasing, jokes, movie references, and impressions. He was also loyal to a fault—if you were one of his boys there was nothing he wouldn't do for you.

"You nervous about John?" Joey asked, referring to my opponent—a southpaw who was twenty pounds bigger, ten years younger, and looked like he belonged in the sport. Unlike myself.

"Me? Not at all," I lied, unconvincingly.

"Remember," Joey said. "You're a martial artist, not a fighter."

"What do you mean by that?" I asked, sensitive to a possible insult.

"A fighter trains to defeat his opponent. A martial artist trains to defeat himself," Joey said. "You're not fighting John. You're fighting yourself."

"Can you tell John that?"

"This smoker is in-house," Joey continued. "All the fighters will be your teammates. So will most of the audience. No need to be nervous. It's just another practice. I want you to gear up. I'm going to walk you through each stage of what will happen tonight, so you'll know what to expect."

"Okay, Coach."

The smoker was an amateur kickboxing match, not MMA, so I put on the more extensive protective gear: shin guards, cup, boxing gloves (what MMA fighters call "the big gloves," as opposed to the four-ounce gloves they usually wear), mouthpiece, and headgear. Almost as useless as a cup is headgear: The minimal extra protection from the padding does not compensate for the loss of peripheral vision. Also, wearing one always made me feel like a dork.

Joey held the pads up for me to punch and kick and repeated

our three-round strategy: "I want you to establish your jab in the first round. Nothing fancy: just jabs. Pop, pop, pop. Keep him at the end of your reach. What's your strength?"

"My length."

"Your strength is your length. Don't let him inside. Make him fear the jab. Then second round, just jabs and crosses for the first half. Keep him at range. Listen to my voice. If it is going well, I'll tell you to let go. Then you hit him with high kicks. You've got crack in that kick. Third round, you knock him out."

"Yes, Coach."

"Breathe, just breathe," Joey continued. "In and out. Deep breaths. When you get tired, what did we work on in practice? What do you tell yourself?"

"I can do this."

"You can do this. You are never going to be more tired than you were that day you sparred the English guy. What was his name, Fred?"

"Chris."

"After two rounds you were kneeling on the ground begging, 'Coach, Coach, let me stop. I can't breathe. I can't fight another round.' You remember?"

"Unfortunately."

"And what did I say to you?"

"'Get your ass off the ground, you old, fat, pussy writer before I put on the gloves and beat you myself.'"

"Ha!" Joey laughed. "No, what did I say?"

"'Do you want an easy fight?'" I said.

"And what did you say?"

"'Easy fight, Coach,'" I said, although truthfully I would have taken a moderately more difficult fight in exchange for some extra rest.

"You've trained hard," Joey said. "So this will be an easy fight."

"Yes, Coach."

"I want you to say this after me: 'There's no place I'd rather be than right here right now.'"

"There's no place I'd rather be than right here right now," I said, trying not to smile. I could think of a lot of places I would have preferred.

"Yeah!" Joey enthused. "Now we're going to walk to the ring. I want you to climb in and circle it. Look strong. First impressions matter. There won't be any judges at this smoker. But you need to practice looking strong for your upcoming MMA fight."

I circled the ring and came over to the corner where Joey was standing.

"I'm running the event," he said. "But I'll be cornering you tonight."

It was quite an honor that of all his students he'd choose to corner me, so I said with sincerity, "Thank you, Coach."

"Listen to my voice. You do as I tell you and you'll be fine. Now I want you to shadowbox for three rounds and listen to my commands."

When the three rounds were over, Joey gave me permission to return home for the afternoon. Covered in sweat, I walked into the lobby and bumped into Randy Couture's son Ryan. The best amateur in the gym, Ryan was looking to turn pro and follow in his father's footsteps. He was fighting in the smoker as well. Fortunately, I didn't have to face him. Every time we had sparred together, he had battered my legs so badly I couldn't walk without a limp for days afterward.

"You ready?" Ryan asked.

"The scary thing is I think Joey wants me to win more than I do,"

I said. "If I fall down, he'll personally drag my ass across the finish line."

"You're lucky to have a coach who cares so much," Ryan said, looking askance at me, ungrateful fool that I was.

"You're right," I agreed. "I'll see you tonight."

I was hoping to relax and clear my mind. Instead, all afternoon was spent clearing my bladder. I was like an eighty-year-old. Every thirty minutes I was running to the bathroom. And these weren't little dribbles; they were wake-up-in-the-morning streams. I'd had stage fright and pre-fight jitters before, but this was ridiculous. I must have lost three pounds in water weight.

Not only did this continue after I returned to Xtreme Couture in the evening, but the pace quickened. Every ten minutes I was pulling my cup down and holding forth. It didn't help that this was the sign above the urinals:

> **IF YOU BLEED OR VOMIT . . .**
> **PLEASE CLEAN UP YOUR MESS**
>
> **THERE ARE LYSOL AND RUBBER GLOVES UNDERNEATH**
> **THE SINK NEAR THE SHAKE MACHINE.**
>
> **—THANKS**

The only relief against my feelings of shame at being so frightened was that I was not the only one repeatedly relieving myself. Another fighter on the night's card, Mike, kept joining me at the next urinal. Then again, he had better reason than me to have a weak bladder: He was matched up against Ryan Couture.

"Been like this all afternoon for you?" I asked.

"Yeah, man," he said. "It's fucking embarrassing."

Joey gathered all the fighters on the second floor. Standing next to him was Randy Couture, wearing an Affliction T-shirt, a major MMA sponsor whose aesthetic style is Goth barf. We all tried not to stare at him. To us he was a living legend: It was like being in the presence of Achilles.

"So we have a special treat for you tonight," Joey said. "Randy has graciously offered to serve as your referee. Do you have anything you'd like to add, Randy?"

"You are all teammates," Randy said. "So be safe and have fun."

As soon as Randy finished speaking, Mike and I ran to the bathroom.

In an effort to calm my nerves, Joey had assigned Carlos (age eight) and his brother Giovani (age seven) as my other cornermen. They were Xtreme Couture's mascots, not because they were so cute (although they were) but because they were so technically skilled in every aspect of the sport. When their doting dad, on his knees, held the pads for them, even the pros would stop and watch. "That's the future of MMA," Joey said to me once. "And it's frightening."

"Yeah," I responded. "They'll be the first generation of MMA fighters who actually like their father."

"Joey says it's time for me to wrap up your gloves," Carlos informed me, holding a roll of athletic tape in his little hands.

"Okay, Carlos," I said.

"You ready?" Joey asked impatiently when my hands were finally wrapped.

I had a problem. I felt yet another urgent need to use the bathroom again, but Carlos had already taped up my gloves. Should I humiliate myself and ask Joey to unwrap my gloves or should I hold it? Was the shame or the discomfort worse?

"Coach, I kinda need to go. Is there time?"

"Is this a real pee?" Joey asked, imitating a kindergarten teacher speaking to a toddler. "Or a nervous pee?"

Trying to save face by making a joke out of it, I said in a little-boy voice, "It's a little nervous pee."

"Let's go."

As I walked toward the ring, more than a little worried I might piss my pants, I wondered, not for the first or last time, how I had gotten myself into this mess.

TAPPED OUT

ACT I

BRAZILIAN JIU-JITSU

CHAPTER 1
Kung Fu Panda

"Matt Polly is like Jet Li, if Jet Li were white and had let himself go."

—JACOB FORTIN, FIGHTLINKER.COM

How did I get myself into this mess?

I was trying to impress a girl.

Em's uncle, Dwight, had invited us to participate in the 2007 Figawi, the first race of the sailing season. (It gets its name from the foggy New England weather of late spring: *Figawi* is Bostonese for "Where the fuck are we?") Our relationship was relatively new, and this was my first introduction to anyone in her family. I wanted to impress, but, being from Kansas, my only naval experiences involved motorboats on ponds. To me, a sailboat is an extremely complicated and expensive horse and buggy. Without an iota of sailing skills, my role on the boat devolved to that of ballast—a fatty on the side.

3

Along with Em and Dwight, our crew consisted of Em's aunt, Bonnie, Em's late-twenties cousin, Phil, and his frat buddy, TG. The weather was perfect, which is to say it was terrible for sailing— sunny and no wind. We had a lot of time to chit-chat. When it came my turn to explain what I did for a living, I said that I had just written a book about the two years I had spent in the early nineties studying kung fu with the Shaolin monks in China.

"That's sort of like the UFC, right?" TG asked me.

"A bit," I said, surprised that he knew about the Ultimate Fighting Championship, the American promotion that had popularized the sport of mixed martial arts (MMA). "I studied *sanda*, which is the Chinese style of kickboxing. The rules are more restrictive. Ground fighting is not allowed."

"So would you fight Chuck Liddell for a million dollars?" he asked excitedly, referring to the UFC's most popular and dominant star at the time.

Now I was shocked.

How does he know about Chuck Liddell?

When I was growing up, the martial arts were a marginal activity—the provenance of geeks and losers, a live-action version of Dungeons and Dragons. I knew about Chuck Liddell because I was one of those martial arts geeks. I had been a big fan of the UFC in the late nineties but had stopped paying attention after it had been banned in forty-seven states. I assumed that the sport had simply fallen off the cultural radar, slipping into the netherworld to take its place next to Toughman and Bumfights.

Somehow a cultural trend in my supposed area of expertise had swept the country (specifically, males under the age of thirty), and I was clueless. It was like the indie band I had followed in high school had gone mainstream behind my back.

I also felt slightly insulted by TG's question. *A million dollars?* Heck, for that much money my mother would fight Chuck Liddell. And if the promoters offered an extra million win bonus, she'd probably take it to a decision. Mama Polly has heavy hands and a wicked right slap.

"I'd do it for a lot less than a million," I scoffed.

"How much?"

"Let's say a hundred grand."

"You think you could beat him?" TG asked, eyes wide.

"No, not a chance," I laughed. "He'd stomp me."

"Then why 100K?"

"Fifty for medical and fifty for pain and suffering."

As our boat inched across the finish line, we tied up in the harbor of Nantucket. Engaging in post-race partying, Phil, TG, Em, and I wandered through the land of gray-slated houses, where white men are not afraid to wear pink but call it Nantucket red. At various intervals the boys would chant, "MMA! MMA! Chuck Liddell! Chuck Liddell!" And as they did, other roving packs of young men would pick up the chorus.

"What's going on?" I asked Phil, feeling like Alice in Wonderland.

"Bro, don't you know? Chuck is fighting Rampage Jackson tonight."

I don't want to get too deep into identity politics, because like Stephen Colbert I don't see race. But Chuck "The Iceman" Liddell was the greatest white hope since Rocky Balboa, while Quinton "Rampage" Jackson, who came up in the Japanese promotion Pride FC, where the line between real fighting and pro wrestling was thin, had developed a Mr. T comic persona. (Hollywood eventually took notice and gave him the Mr. T role in the movie *The A-Team*.) Fighting has always been a tribal sport.

After dinner, we gathered to watch the fight. This was not only a rematch but a chance for redemption. In 2003, Chuck Liddell had gone to Japan to prove that the American UFC had superior fighters to Japan's Pride FC. It did not. More than sixty-seven thousand fans showed up to the Tokyo Dome (the biggest audience the UFC had drawn up to that point was fourteen thousand) and saw Jackson rough Liddell up for two rounds until Liddell's corner finally threw in the towel. Since then, Liddell had rolled off seven highlight-reel knockout victories in a row, making him, with his signature mohawk, the most popular MMA fighter in America.

He certainly was in that room. The boys were pumped. "Chuck Liddell! Chuck Liddell!" Personally, I had a soft spot for Rampage. In the pre-fight promotional package, he had the funniest trash-talking line: "When the time comes, I'm gonna break The Ice. You feel me? That's how I do. I'm an icebreaker."

And so on May 26, 2007, the announcers primed the pay-per-view audience for the main event—the light heavyweight (205 pounds) championship. Longtime play-by-play announcer Mike Goldberg, color commentator Joe Rogan (of *Fear Factor* fame), and expert analyst and heavyweight champion Randy Couture lined up in front of the camera to give their opinions. Joe Rogan leaned toward Liddell: "He can end a fight at any second. He's got knockout power in his hands and feet." Randy differed: "I believe Rampage can beat Chuck."

Knowledgeable fans might have viewed Randy's opinion as sour grapes, since Chuck had recently beaten him twice at light heavyweight, sending him into a brief retirement before Randy came back, like the Crypt Keeper, jumped a weight class, and won the heavyweight (265 pounds) title. But Randy had proven to be such an accurate prognosticator that gamblers often waited for his predictions before placing their bets.

As fifteen thousand fans at the MGM Grand in Las Vegas cheered, the room went dark. When the lights came back on, Quinton "Rampage" Jackson strutted down the aisle, sporting a massive chain around his neck. At intervals, he stopped and howled at the ceiling like a wolf. The crowd at the MGM and in our TV room booed his pro wrestling theatrics. He stopped and took off his shirt and hat in front of the Octagon, an eight-post, black chain-link-fence cage that has become a symbol and trademark of the sport.

The lights went down again and then came up spooky white with dry-ice machines covering the arena in smoke for The Iceman. He sauntered in wearing an Affliction T-shirt with a skull and skeletal bat wings across it. As he took off his shirt, he revealed a mini–Buddha belly that made many question his conditioning. He seemed to be spending more time at Hollywood nightclubs than the gym.

The tale of the tape popped up on the TV screen. Chuck had the longer reach advantage (six inches), but Rampage had youth (he was twenty-eight, compared to Chuck's thirty-seven).

Chuck was bouncing on his toes while Rampage paced back and forth. The announcer, Bruce "Veteran Voice of the Octagon" Buffer, stepped to center stage. No one is better at revving up a crowd with nothing more than his voice, except perhaps for his older brother, Michael Buffer, who is boxing's most famous announcer. After plugging the UFC's budget list of sponsors (Xenergy, Toyo Tires, and *Hostel: Part II*; it was still early in the UFC's ascendance into social acceptability), Bruce opened with a few of the licensed and registered family catchphrases: "Ladies and gentlemen, this is the main event of the evening! This is the moment you've all been waiting for! It's TIIIIMMME!"

To the center of the ring stepped "Big" John McCarthy, the sport's most popular referee. He waved the two fighters to the center of the ring for the stare-down, a ritual where each guy tries to psych out the other. Rampage Jackson leaned in close and made growling faces, which caused Chuck to smirk.

"All right, gentlemen, you received your instruction in the locker room. We want a good, clean, hard fight," Big John McCarthy said, and then continued with a couple of rhetorical questions. "Do I have any questions from the challenger? Do I have any questions from the champion? I want you to touch gloves, fight clean, fight hard, fight fair. Step back. Let's get this going."

They touched gloves and returned to their corners.

"Are you ready?" Big John asked Rampage, who nodded. "Are you ready?" Big John asked Chuck, who nodded. Big John clapped his hands and shouted his famous catchphrase: "Let's get it on!"

It is traditional when the round begins for the two fighters to stick out a fist and bump gloves again, but Chuck skipped the niceties and fired a jab at Rampage's face instead. Chuck then circled and backed away using a great deal of footwork to stay outside of Rampage's range. He tossed in a few jabs and low kicks to keep Rampage at bay. He was forcing Rampage to be the aggressor, to follow him, so he could play the role with which he was most comfortable: the counter-striker. As both fighters were feeling each other out, trying to gauge the other's rhythm, Chuck made a fatal mistake.

One minute and thirteen seconds into the fight, Chuck threw a lazy left hook to Rampage's body that he left hanging. Rampage responded with a right hook to Chuck's unprotected chin. Chuck's body folded underneath him. Rampage dropped down and delivered four more punches to Chuck's head as his body went limp and flat like a drunk passing out. Big John McCarthy pulled Rampage off of Chuck. And as quickly as that, The Iceman's reign was over.

Unlike in boxing, where top earners are carefully protected, in MMA even the champions lose. One moment you are a star, the next you are seeing stars, and the next you are dancing with the stars.

UFC color commentator Joe Rogan shouted, "Unbelievable!"

UFC play-by-play announcer Mike Goldberg shouted, "Liddell is in disbelief!"

The sentiment was shared by the boys in the room. On his feet, Phil shouted at the TV: "He took a dive! He took a dive! That's bullshit! He threw the fight!"

"No he didn't," I said. "Rampage caught him on the button."

"Button? What? There's no such thing as a button! He took a dive!"

As the UFC ran the replay, Randy Couture said, "There's the right hook. Right on the button."

"Oh," Phil said, sitting down. "I guess there is a button."

"Sure . . . ," I grumbled. "When Randy says it, you believe it."

"So where's the button?" Phil asked.

"Both are located about an inch or so to the left and right of the tip of the chin," I said, reaching for another beer.

"There are two buttons?"

"Think of them more like a metaphor. The buttons are the two spots on the human head that require the least amount of force to cause a knockout."

"Okay . . ."

"If you nail those spots with a hook, the skull whiplashes, like, say, in a car crash, right?

"All right . . ."

"The brain pinballs inside the skull and goes into failsafe mode. It shuts down higher functions, like consciousness, to preserve more critical ones, like breathing. So tap the button: lights out."

"So Chuck didn't take a dive?"

"No," I said. "But his market value just crashed."

■ ■ ■

Several weeks later I was playing no-limit Texas hold 'em with a group of friends. Sitting next to me was my book editor, Patrick. As my chips dribbled away along with my *Rounders* fantasy of sitting at the World Series of Poker's final table, I decided it might be better to focus on my real career. I was in love. I wanted to get married. I needed another assignment.

"How about mysticism?" I said, pitching Patrick on my big idea for my next book. "The idea is I'll go study and live with different masters of different faiths—Zen priests, Trappist monks, the Sufis. What do you think?"

"Hmm, yeah, that's ahh, hmm," Patrick replied, staring hard at his cards.

I was crushed. This was my big idea. I didn't really have a plan B. My brain wildly spurted out half-baked ideas.

"How about a book about the influence of Japanese manga on American comic books? I could start with Frank Miller's Wolverine miniseries . . ."

Boring.

"Video game addiction . . ."

Eh.

"Poker?"

Already been done.

"How about MMA?" I finally asked in desperation. "It's gotten to be huge with guys your age. And yet most of them don't even understand the basics of fighting. I could do a history of the sport, maybe some cultural analysis."

"That's it," Patrick said with eyes so bright I realized I'd stumbled upon yet another eighteen- to thirty-four-year-old MMA fan.

"Great!" I said, before something in his expression made me worry. "But . . . you don't want a participatory book? I mean, you don't expect me to get into the cage, do you?"

"Of course! That's a great idea!"

"Patrick, I haven't trained or fought competitively in fifteen years. I'm thirty-six. My idea of exercise is walking to the fridge for another beer."

"Exactly. You're like all the guys who will buy this book. Out-of-shape ex-athletes who dream about competing again one last time."

"So you want me to be like Bernie Mac in *Mr. 3000*?"

"How long would you need to get back into fighting shape?"

"Like a decade."

"How about a year?"

"Not a chance."

"Two?"

"I'm not sure I have the heart for it anymore," I said. "When I was twenty I thought I was invincible. Now I know what can go wrong."

"Overcoming that fear will be what your book is about."

"Let me get this straight," I said. "The only way I get the job is if I get in the cage?"

"Correct."

"Oh, fuck me."

■ ■ ■

The reaction from friends and family was universally negative.

"Dude, you must be nuts. UFC?!?!" e-mailed my best buddy from college. "You do realize that we're entering our late thirties here, don't you? Write by all means, and train if you must, but don't hop in the ring with those maniacs. I personally really enjoy your sense of humor as it currently is—i.e., without brain damage."

"Why are you doing this to me again?" my mother cried. I had put her through the emotional wringer when I left college more than fifteen years back to study kung fu with the Shaolin monks in China, and she still wasn't over it.

"Mom, how can I fairly or accurately write about these MMA fighters if I'm not willing to walk a mile in their shoes? Anybody can slap a few interviews together and call it a book. It takes real courage to get in the cage."

"I can't even speak to you about this," she said as she handed the phone to my father.

My father, who prides himself on his rationality, tried to reason with me. "Son, the human race has been evolving toward more aquiline features. But these MMA guys—"

"It's not evolution; they just train harder than anyone else."

"I know I didn't give you much of a body," my father continued. "But I did give you a pretty good brain. Why risk one on the frail hope of the other?"

"I think you've answered your question."

■ ■ ■

When I was a young man and change seemed easy, I had a to-do list inside my head, titled "Things That Are Wrong with Matt." As I aged, this to-do list slowly morphed into a procrastination list. For nearly a decade it read:

THINGS THAT MATT SHOULD DO STARTING TOMORROW BUT PROBABLY WON'T

1) Make money
2) Establish a writing career
3) Find a serious girlfriend
4) Marry her
5) Start a family
6) Get healthy
   a) Exercise more
   b) Eat smarter
   c) Drink less

When my first book came out, I was finally able to scratch off (1) and (2). Soon afterward, I met Em, clubbed her over the head, and dragged her back to my cave. That took care of (3). Now all I needed to do was get healthy and get Em to marry me and start a family.

I'm not sure which scared me more. As for getting healthy, I knew I needed to change my lifestyle, but I didn't really want to. I was an ex–martial artist who had fallen off the path of righteousness. But I was also a nearly middle-aged man who had let himself go. I weighed 250 pounds and my blood pressure was 145/100. I was a cardiac arrest waiting to happen.

Change is painful. But MMA is more painful.

There is little room to slack or procrastinate with MMA. It's a zero-sum sport whose motivational toolbox is all sticks and no carrots—*The MMA Diet Book: Exercise More and Eat Less or Get Your Ass Beat*. The anguish of defeat in combat sports is primal. Two men enter; one man leaves with his ego and body intact.

When I finally asked Em what she thought about this idea, she said in her practical way, "Given long-term health considerations, a broken nose is far better than a beer gut."

It was ironic that a sport once considered so brutal that it was banned in forty-seven states might actually save my life.

CHAPTER 2
Descendants of Hercules: MMA 101

"Anybody fights me

I'll bust him wide open and crush his bones.

Better have his next of kin standing by

To carry him out when I'm through."

—EPEIUS, *THE ILIAD*

I should have made a beeline to the nearest gym. My body was a shipwreck, and I had fifteen years of barnacles to scrape off. Instead, I decided to burn a month researching the history of mixed martial arts—reading every book and article on the subject and watching every UFC video. I may be crap as a fighter, but I am an expert at surfing the Web, lying on the couch, and watching bad TV.

One thing I learned is that watching MMA fights eight hours a day for four weeks is a really bad idea. You get an event-by-event, injury-by-injury list of all the horrible things that can happen and have happened to much harder men than you. It gave me blood-soaked nightmares. I woke up screaming: "Tap!" And the absolute last thing I wanted to do was start training.

The rest of what I learned is summarized below.

■ ■ ■

Not content merely with philosophy, drama, comedy, science, or democracy, the ancient Greeks also invented MMA. Wrestling was introduced into their Olympics in 708 BCE and boxing in 688 BCE. It is not clear who had the bright idea of combining both boxing and wrestling like chocolate and peanut butter, but mixed martial arts, which they called *pankration* ("all powers"), became an Olympic sport in 648 BCE. It took the world more than twenty-five hundred years to rediscover the idea.

All three combat sports were practiced by the Greek elite. Plato was famed for his wrestling skill. In fact, some scholars believe that Plato's real name was Aristocles, and that "Plato" was a jock nickname (roughly, "the broad") derived either from the size of his forehead or the girth of his penis. Plato was Greek, and the Greeks liked to wrestle in the nude and not always platonically.

In terms of rules, style, and content, ancient *pankration* would be familiar to fans of today's MMA. Contestants could punch, kick, elbow, and knee any part of the body; they could clinch, throw, trip, arm bar, leg lock, and choke. Victory was achieved only when one opponent couldn't continue or surrendered by raising a finger: the ancient equivalent of tapping out. And like Epeius in *The Iliad*, *pankratiasts* talked trash just like many modern MMA tough guys.

The origins of modern MMA began in late nineteenth-century Japan with Jigoro Kano, the founder of judo. He was a small, frail boy who was often picked on by bullies—a common archetype in martial arts history. After graduating from Tokyo Imperial University, Kano became an influential educator.

Kano transformed traditional Japanese martial arts, with its focus on battlefield combat, into a civilian sport. He removed the most injurious techniques of the classical styles—the strikes, the biting, the eye gouging, the ball busting—and left the relatively safe ones: throws and pins. From an educator's point of view, it made perfect sense. No teacher wants to explain to Mrs. Tanaka why little Riku lost an eye in PE class.

Adopted by the Japanese public school system (1911), judo became so popular it was made an Olympic sport in 1964. Kano's students were so successful in exporting the sport that judo became for a short period of time America's, Brazil's, and Russia's most popular martial art. Kano's envoy to Brazil was Mitsuyo Maeda, who arrived in 1914.

Maeda's entrée into Brazilian society was assisted by Gastao Gracie, a prominent businessman. In return for the help, Maeda offered to teach his art to Gastao's sons Carlos and Helio, the latter of whom was yet another fragile and sickly boy in the history of martial arts. Helio was forbidden from training and had to learn by watching from the sidelines. One day Carlos was late to teach a class, so Helio stepped in and was so good that the students asked him to continue.

Still weak and frail, Helio modified Maeda's style to focus on ground fighting and leverage in a way that would have made Archimedes proud: "Give me a long enough lever and a fulcrum, and I shall move the world." Helio's adjustments were the basis for what was to become known as the distinct style of Brazilian jiu-jitsu (BJJ). And his philosophy tapped into the underlying hope that attracts nerds like me to the martial arts: Superior skill and technique can defeat superior size and strength.

Helio and his brother proved this point by publicly offering to fight anyone at anytime in *vale tudo* ("anything goes") contests. As Helio defeated one bigger and stronger fighter after another, the Gracie Challenge made the family and their style famous through-out Brazil. But it was one of Helio's very few defeats that won him his greatest glory.

Hearing of Gracie's fame, Japan's best judo player, Masahiko Kimura, traveled to Brazil in 1951 to take up the gauntlet. Twenty thousand people showed up to watch. The much larger Kimura threw Helio around but could not finish him. At the thirteen-minute mark, Helio made a mistake and Kimura applied a shoulder lock. What happened next is best summarized by Kimura himself:

> I thought he would surrender immediately. But Helio would not tap the mat. I had no choice but to keep on twisting the arm. The stadium became quiet. The bone of his arm was coming close to the breaking point. Finally, the sound of bone breaking echoed throughout the stadium. Helio still did not surrender. His left arm was already powerless. Under the rules, I had no choice but to twist the arm again. Another bone was broken. Helio still did not tap. When I tried to twist the arm once more, a white towel was thrown in. I won by TKO.

While Helio's elbow was dislocated and the radius and ulna bones were broken, his family's reputation was immortalized. The newspaper's front-page headline was MORAL VICTORY FOR HELIO GRACIE. He became a national hero, and his family's style of fighting Brazil's most popular martial art. Today it seems like every street in Rio and São Paulo has a jiu-jitsu studio.

Their fathers having conquered Brazil, Carlos's and Helio's sons decided to spread the good word to America. It was not easy.

America's past combat tradition rested almost exclusively in striking—boxing and Bruce Lee—not grappling. To the average American's perspective, pro wrestling was fake and amateur wrestling was boring. A bunch of Brazilians rolling around on the ground did not immediately impress. And so the Gracies advertised their open challenge. Those few who foolishly accepted were soundly trounced. A journalist caught wind and wrote an article about the Gracie Challenge for *Playboy*.

Art Davie, an advertising executive and entrepreneur (his latest venture was XARM, a short-lived hybrid sport that combined kickboxing and arm wrestling), read the article and contacted Rorion Gracie, the eldest son of Helio, about turning their open challenge into a TV show. The idea was to invite masters of various styles to compete in a single-elimination tournament to decide which fighting style was best. It would be a live-action version of every thirteen-year-old boy's fantasy debate: Who would win in a fight between Bruce Lee and Hulk Hogan, Iron Man and the Incredible Hulk, Muhammad Ali and Antonio Inoki?

Turned down by the big boys at HBO and Showtime, they found a pay-per-view partner in SEG, a low-rent production company specializing in offbeat events like the mixed-gender tennis match between Jimmy Connors and Martina Navratilova. Rorian Gracie's student, John Milius, the screenwriter of *Apocalypse Now*,

Conan the Barbarian, and *Red Dawn*, came up with idea of using an octagon-shaped cage. (Fortunately, his idea to surround the cage with an alligator-infested moat was not implemented.)

Named the Ultimate Fighting Championship, the entire carnival slinked into Denver, Colorado, on November 12, 1993. It was the perfect location because, to quote MMA journalist Jake Rossen, Denver had "no athletic commission to intervene, [but] plenty of limited-liability coverage." Among the eight contestants were a Dutch kickboxer, an American who wrestled professionally in Japan, a 410-pound sumo wrestler, a boxer who decided to wear only one glove, and the Gracie family representative, Royce Gracie. He was selected ahead of his many talented brothers and cousins because at barely 160 pounds he looked more like an accountant than a barroom bully. The family wanted to prove that Gracie jiu-jitsu was so superior it could defeat bigger and stronger experts of other fighting arts.

It's usually best not to enter a tournament in which one of the contestant's brothers owns a stake in the promotional company. None of the other participants had any experience with *vale tudo*, whereas the Gracie family had been fighting and winning contests like this for fifty years. There were no judges, no weight classes, no time limits, and only two rules: no biting and no eye gouging.

Royce Gracie, the smallest man in the contest, blew through his opponents with ease. His victory and his family's previously little-known style blew the minds of the American martial arts community. Gracie jiu-jitsu schools expanded rapidly with new members, and the modest popularity and profitability of the event convinced the promoters to make the UFC a regular affair. The world of martial arts would never be the same again.

The success of the UFC inspired the Japanese, who have never met an American invention they didn't want to copy and then perfect. The Yakuza (Japanese mafia) started up their own promotion, Pride Fighting Championship, in 1997. (I once asked Mark Coleman, a famous Pride FC champion, if the organization was really run by the Yakuza. We were at a Buffalo Wild Wings franchise in the suburbs of Chicago, but, before answering, Coleman looked over his right shoulder, then looked over his left shoulder, then nodded almost imperceptibly and mouthed the word *yes*.)

If MMA was a cult curiosity in America, it became a phenomenon in Japan. The fighters became celebrities with their own shaving cream commercials. One of Pride FC's biggest shows had ninety thousand Japanese in attendance. And the TV ratings in Japan were through the roof: One Pride FC New Year's event had half the country watching.

In contrast, the UFC was lucky if it could convince five thousand people to show up, and they were not the kind of people any corporate sponsor would want to reach. Compared to Japan's quiet, respectful middle-class audiences, the UFC crowds were the Roman mob. "It was like a Hell's Angels convention," Mark Jacobs, a columnist for *Black Belt* magazine, told me. "Actually, a Hell's Angels convention would have been a step up." At UFC 8: David vs. Goliath, a riot broke out in the audience and several popular fighters were involved.

This event began the political backlash in America against the sport, which in retrospect seems absurd. If it's okay for two men to box and it's okay for two men to wrestle, why is it wrong for two men to be allowed to do both at the same time? But the blame largely belongs to the UFC's management, who were marketing MMA not as a sport but as a spectacle. Before every show the announcer would emphasize that "there were no rules" and anything could happen, "even death."

Some anti-UFC protestors sent a compilation videotape of the promotion's worst moments—and there were more than a few—to Senator John McCain and hit pay dirt. There is no group of people who hate MMA more than old boxers. It threatens their entire worldview about what constitutes a fair fight and revolts them on an aesthetic and moral level. ("My God, you can't hit a man when he's down. What would the Marquess of Queensberry think?") John McCain, who boxed at the U.S. Naval Academy, called MMA "human cockfighting."

Soon, forty-seven states had banned the sport—putting MMA in the category of medical marijuana and gay marriage. In 1997 McCain became chairman of the Senate Commerce Committee, which oversees the cable industry. Coincidentally, all the major cable companies—TCI, Time Warner, Cablevision—pulled the plug on the UFC. Of course, they still programmed porn, but MMA was beyond the pale, marking the first time in America's puritanical history that sex trumped violence.

Cut off from the television lights, the UFC entered what hardcore fans call "the Dark Ages." Desperate, management reversed course by cutting a deal with New Jersey (i.e., Atlantic City) to re-legalize the sport in return for accepting their athletic commission's oversight and adopting medical and drug testing for the fighters and a more extensive set of rules—thirty-one in total, of which my three favorites are no pinching ("That tickles"), no abusive language ("Yo mamma is so fat"), and no putting a finger into any orifice ("That tickles").

All of these changes were a crucial step in transforming MMA from a spectacle into a sport, but for the owners of the UFC it was too little too late. Into the breach stepped Dana White, a Las Vegas native whose life had more than its fair share of failure. An amateur boxer who didn't have the heart to turn pro, he had been reduced to teaching boxercize classes—a fact that envious media types will never let him forget. Seeing an opportunity in the floundering promotion, the alternatively charming, obnoxious, and profane White convinced Tito Ortiz and Chuck Liddell— two of the few stars the UFC had left—to let him be their manager. While negotiating on their behalf, Dana discovered what dire financial straits the UFC was in. When the owners were forced to sell, he was ready to pounce.

Dana had previously introduced two of his high school friends, Frank and Lorenzo Fertitta, to the excitement of MMA. The Fertitta brothers are the third generation of an Italian American family to operate a Vegas casino empire. In 2001, they bought this crazy fighting promotion for two million dollars, gave this loud-mouthed Irish kid Dana White a ten percent stake to oversee it, and together turned the UFC into the most legitimate, scandal-free organization in MMA. (Their tough Italian ancestors must be turning in their graves to see that their progeny have three hundred of the world's best leg breakers under contract but use them only for legal purposes.)

With New Jersey as the example, Dana White lobbied, state by state, to end MMA's prohibition period. In his charm offensive, he focused on the safety record of the sport. Unlike in boxing, football, or marathon running, there had been no deaths or serious injuries. While gladiatorial imagery was freely used in promotions, it became clearer that MMA was light-years from the

Colosseum. After all, gladiators were slaves who were forced to fight with weapons to the death. Their careers didn't include a retirement plan. MMA fighters were free men voluntarily participating in a regulated, unarmed combat sport that at worst resulted in a broken hand or a concussion. Sure, there were plenty of bruises and blood, but almost all the wounds were superficial and easily healed. MMA wasn't as safe as golf, but it wasn't Mexican knife fighting. Even John McCain changed positions (as he did later on immigration), grumpily admitting that the sport had cleaned up its act.

The political success was not, however, matched on the financial front. Dana White improved the quality of his talent pool and even had a few genuine stars on the roster, but he couldn't compete with all the laundered cash the Yakuza-run Pride FC threw at top talent. A bitter joke among employees was that UFC stood for "U Fight for Cheap." Despite his passion and impressive carnival barker skill, Dana was barely able to uptick the sport's popularity in America. Curling had more fans.

The Fertittas continued to funnel good money after bad into the UFC to keep the promotion afloat. Best estimates are they lost ten to twelve million dollars a year for four years, making them officially the best high school buddies anyone has ever had. (Mine bought me a steak and some lap dances at my bachelor party.) Even Lorenzo, who is the company's good cop, was considering cutting his losses. And then, like good sons of Vegas, they opted instead to go all in.

Their river card was a reality TV show, *The Ultimate Fighter*, produced in 2005. It was like *American Idol* meets *Survivor* and dry humps *Jersey Shore*. Sixteen up-and-coming MMA fighters were stuck in a house with no TV, no magazines, no books, but plenty of booze. Each week, two men entered the Octagon and one man left the show. The coaches were the UFC's most popular and personable stars, Chuck Liddell and Randy Couture.

No channel wanted it. MMA was still too obscure and too toxic. What advertiser dared to be associated with a sport that was still illegal in half the country? The Fertitta brothers had to put their own money down to pay for the production, estimated to be ten million dollars. Even then they were only able to give it away for free to Spike TV, the male-centric cable channel whose bread and butter was pro wrestling, *Star Trek* reruns, and James Bond marathons.

The Ultimate Fighter was a surprise hit, a compelling and captivating examination of an unknown, tortured, and talented group of young men aspiring to better their lives through grit, determination, and the power of TV. Almost overnight, American males under the age of thirty turned into rabid MMA fans. A new generation had found its new sport.

But the surge in popularity might have been a flash in the pan without the finale, which Dana White calls the most important fight in the history of the UFC. Stephan Bonnar, a personal trainer from Chicago, and Forrest Griffin, a college-educated police officer from Athens, Georgia, put on the kind of gutsy, tenacious, courage-and-skill, heart-stopping, back-and-forth, never-say-die war that makes sportswriters declare "fight of the century" and fans call all their friends: "You have to see this!" The closest I've ever seen to anything like it in my lifetime was the trilogy between Arturo Gatti and Micky Ward.

Bonnar and Griffin also happened to be two well-educated, well-spoken white guys with sharp senses of humor. In the pre-fight promo material, the self-deprecating Forrest thanked his coaches: "Because without them I probably would have actually gone to law school and be a police lieutenant or something somewhere, have a beautiful wife, kid, white picket fence. But thanks to them, I live in their living room on a mattress and I don't have medical insurance and I get beat up for a living."

UFC attendance and ticket prices went through the roof, as did the core of their business model: pay-per-view. MMA became the hottest new sport in the country. Bought for two million dollars, the UFC was now estimated to be worth one billion dollars. The boxercize instructor was now the One Hundred Million Dollar Man.

It was the kind of overwhelming overnight success that even grudging media types had to respect and cover. And if any publication resisted, Dana White, hallowed be his name, either bullied it into submission or bought so many advertising pages that the editors rolled over and had their tummies rubbed. Multiple glowing puff pieces appeared in *Playboy, Esquire, Sports Illustrated, Rolling Stone*, etc.

It was this carrot-and-stick approach that White used mercilessly against his competition. When other promoters, seeing the MMA gold rush, started rival promotions in America, Dana badgered, sued, and counter-programmed them into bankruptcy. When stories circulated in the Japanese press of the Yakuza's involvement in the Pride FC and the Fuji network terminated their television contract, the UFC bought Pride FC at a cut rate and acquired the contracts for the rest of the world's best MMA fighters. In one stroke, the UFC became the Windows operating system of MMA and Dana White its profane Bill Gates.

Whether it is good for the sport that one man has near total monopolistic control is a subject of much debate. But it is unlikely there will be much of a challenge anytime soon. As of this writing, the last minor thorn in Dana White's side was a California promotion called Strikeforce, which had a TV deal with Showtime and CBS. Unable to knock them out, he simply bought them out. And now Dana White, hallowed be his name, reigns supreme.

CHAPTER 3
Gracies Don't Tap

"The whole idea of building the UFC was to prove
that Gracie jiu-jitsu was the best martial art and
fighting style."

—ROYCE GRACIE

New Yorkers have a soundtrack looping in their heads called
"Gotta Make the Rent." I first heard the music after living in the
city for six months. One day I put my debit card into a Chase
ATM, and the machine told me my checking account was negative. Then it ate my card. I was in shock. It was like someone had
seized my middle-class passport. Chest heaving, hands trembling,
I walked inside to the customer service rep and explained to him
as calmly as I could that clearly someone had been stealing from
my account. He printed up my bank records. Sure enough, someone had been stealing from me. That person was me.

Few people feel the pressure to make the rent in NYC more intensely than gym owners. Boxing gyms are space-intensive but tend to attract the poorest of the poor. Even martial arts studios, which appeal to a more affluent clientele, struggle to survive in three-story walk-ups the size of phone booths. Nail salons are a far more lucrative use of floor space.

One of the few exceptions in Manhattan was the Renzo Gracie Academy. A card-carrying member of the Gracie clan, Renzo was both a legendary fighter and widely considered to be the most charming member of the family. His school was the perfect place to start my journey into the world of MMA.

For a month, I had procrastinated going to Renzo's school—I needed just one more day to complete my research, and one more day, and one more day—but the "Rent" song finally became so loud in my head that it pushed me passed my fear and out of my apartment door. So one sweltering August afternoon, I jumped off the E train at Penn Station and walked to the Academy for the free introductory class. It was located in one of those old Manhattan buildings that was built in the era when architects believed brass fixtures and pink marble looked good together. I walked down to the poorly ventilated basement to find three huge (by Manhattan standards) rooms painted white with blue mats covering the floors.

One of the school's instructors, Magno, led me to the corner of the main training room for the intro class/sales pitch. The rest of the room was "rolling" (or as the Japanese call it, *randori*). This is when two training partners wrestle on the ground, each seeking to submit the other. My initial impression was that it looked like a very aggressive game of Twister.

Good-naturedly, Magno explained and demonstrated the

general concepts of Brazilian jiu-jitsu. The goal of the art is simple: Force your opponent to voluntarily give up (submit) by making him an offer he can't refuse. However, unlike in MMA, striking—punches, elbows, knees, and kicks—is forbidden in BJJ. So the three methods available to you are chokes (submit or you will pass out), locks (submit or your elbow, shoulder, knee, etc. will break), and cranks (submit or the pain will get much worse). All of these can be done to a standing opponent but are much easier to accomplish on the ground, where movement is restricted. And so in a fight, the jiu-jitsu practitioner wants to "take the fight to the ground."

Magno asked me to stand so he could show me the "three phases of unarmed combat."

"Is that really necessary?" I asked.

"I go gentle with you."

The first phase is called free movement because both opponents are standing and neither has a hold on the other, allowing them to move freely in any direction. They can punch, kick, or—my favorite—run away. Boxing and kickboxing matches take place almost exclusively in this phase.

"Punch me," Magno said.

I hesitated. I've studied with enough martial arts instructors to know from painful experience that when one says "punch me" it never ends well. With great trepidation, I threw a very slow, telegraphed jab. Magno easily ducked it, grabbed my wrist with one hand and hugged me around the back with the other.

This is the second phase of unarmed combat—often referred to as the clinch. Since one or both opponents have a hold on the other, movement is now restricted.

Almost instantaneously, Magno turned and tossed me over his hip. Flying through the air, I thought that I should have listened to my father and gone to med school. Fortunately, Magno was a gentle soul and it was his job to sell me a membership, so he cradled my body and braced my fall right before I hit the ground. As I lay on my back, he dropped his chest over mine and flattened his body.

This is the third, or ground fighting, phase of unarmed combat, where BJJ stylists live and breathe. In many schools, training partners will start on their knees, simply skipping phases one and two. As the Gracies like to say, "Ninety percent of fights end up on the ground." They have a point. But as Robert Drysdale, one the top three BJJ stylists in the world, later said to me, "True, but one hundred percent of fights start on the feet."

Faster than I could react, Magno grabbed my wrist, put a knee on my chest, threw his other leg over my face, pinned my arm between his knees, leaned back, hyperextended my elbow, and stopped just before the breaking point. Tapping his leg repeatedly with my free hand, I submitted.

"You see, you had to tap," Magno said. "The fight is over and no one is hurt. Jiu-jitsu is the gentle art."

"I see," I said, rubbing my elbow. "And what if I hadn't tapped out?"

"Then your elbow pop, pop, pops," he said. "And you must visit doctor."

"Like that fight in Japan where Renzo refused to tap," I said, recalling a match between Renzo Gracie and Japan's legendary champion Kazushi Sakuraba. Late in the contest, Sakuraba caught Renzo in a *kimura* (shoulder lock). Just like his great uncle Helio, Renzo refused to surrender and had his arm broken. When asked by reporters why he refused to tap, Renzo said, "Honestly, I thought I could still win with one arm."

"The Gracies are special," Magno said. "And a little crazy."

The introductory class was coming to an end, but before it was over Magno wanted to impress a larger point on me.

"You can never understand all of jiu-jitsu," Magno said. "Maybe I grasp sixty percent of it. Jiu-jitsu is always evolving, improving . . ."

He continued on for several more minutes about the mystical nature of BJJ. It felt like a sermon at the Church of Gracie Jiu-Jitsu of Latter Day Saints.

"Last year I invented a move," Magno said with pride. "It never ends."

Inventing a new technique, I'd learn, was one of the highest accomplishments in jiu-jitsu. Unlike in many traditional martial arts, which tend to be backward looking—an ancient master had already perfected the style and it was your job to memorize it— jiu-jitsu is a progressive art. It could be improved.

Our intro class done, I was ushered into the main office—two desks, computers, and chairs—for the final sale. Max, an ex– Boston College football player, explained the financials. A one-year contract was two hundred fifty dollars a month—pricey even by Manhattan standards.

I explained that I intended to study in Manhattan for only six months before traveling to Las Vegas to train at Xtreme Couture, the MMA gym of Randy Couture. I knew six months wasn't enough to even get a basic understanding of the art, but I had a time limit for the book, and it was my assignment to study at various gyms.

"That's too bad," he said. "It takes about six months before students have their first big breakthrough."

"How many students do you have?"

"Too many. More than a thousand. I'm thinking of renting the floor above."

A thousand students was an astronomical number for a single martial arts studio. The Gracies reminded me of what James Michener said about the Christian missionaries who went to Hawaii: "They'd come to do good and did very well indeed."

Having signed the contract, my next expenditure was for a jiu-jitsu *gi*, which is a reinforced and padded karate uniform. Jiu-jitsu can be practiced with or without a *gi*, and there is much debate about which is the better way to train. *Gi* jiu-jitsu is generally considered more technical—with all the clothing to grab, it takes more skill to achieve a submission. Without a *gi*, athletic ability plays a larger role because it is harder to hold on to a sweaty body. At Renzo's, beginning students were expected to train with a *gi* for at least a year before they could advance to the no-*gi* classes.

Having made my purchase, my inner American consumer left the school in a happy mood. The best part of starting any new hobby is buying the equipment. My closet is filled with the leftovers from exercise programs I started and quickly gave up, like Bowflex, Ab Blaster, and Shake Weight.

Heading toward the subway, I made it two blocks before I stepped off a curb and felt a sharp pain in my left ankle. I hadn't twisted it, but the pain was intense. After I hobbled home, I tested my ankle. It creaked like a rusty door. I called my father, an orthopedic surgeon, for an insurance-free consultation.

"You have tendinitis," my father said.

"How could my ankle have that?" I asked. "I haven't used it for anything but walking in ten years."

"You're getting old."

"How long?"

"If you don't stress it, two weeks."

When I told the diagnosis to Em, she asked, "You sure you don't have tendinitis of the head?"

"It's probably psychosomatic," I said. "But maybe God just doesn't want me to train for the next two weeks."

"How did I end up with you?"

"Masochism? Low self-esteem?"

Whatever the reason, I knew she loved me, because every time I limped past her, she would try very, very hard to hide her smirk.

■ ■ ■

Exactly two weeks from my diagnosis, my ankle healed. The next evening I gingerly set out for Renzo's gym for my first day of practice.

As I watched the earlier sessions, psyching myself for my eight o'clock, I was amazed at what a well-oiled machine Renzo's school was. Dozens of students marched into the six o'clock class, which started on time and ended at exactly seven o'clock, and were replaced with a new bunch a few minutes later. The Brazilians, bless their hearts, are not renowned for their dedication to punctuality. Everybody loves Renzo, but he was notorious for agreeing to an engagement only to fail to show up. As for his academy, he was like the Tom Sawyer of MMA, always charming someone else into painting the fence. After six months of nearly never seeing him at his flagship gym, I asked one of his coaches what exactly Renzo did at the school. "Collect the money" was the reply.

But the highlight for the BJJ students was the capoeira class, which was held in one of the smaller rooms. Resembling a precursor to break dancing, capoeira is the only martial art created by slaves. According to legend, the slaves would gather in a circle (*roda*) to play music. Two fighters would enter the circle to spar, but if the master or his minions came to examine what was happening, the fighters would switch back to dancing.

While generally considered an inferior fighting style to jiu-jitsu, capoeira is an undeniably beautiful and graceful art. More importantly, it attracts beautiful and graceful people. Renzo's jiu-jitsu classes were filled with a motley crew of young men. The capoeira classes were dominated by model-thin beauties who looked liked they'd just flown in first class from the runways of Rio for a photo shoot in Manhattan.

Before jiu-jitsu classes started, nearly every guy in a jiu-jitsu *gi* had his face pressed against the window, staring with open mouths at the capoeira women.

"I always come at this time of night, so I can ogle," said one.

"What's the chance I'm ever going to get into a street fight?" a Japanese guy with Rastafarian dreadlocks asked his friend. "Explain to me why am I rolling around with sweaty guys when I could be in there with them."

"Stop looking at the capoeira class," Magno, the instructor from my introductory class, shouted.

I filed in with the rest of the average-looking people into the white belt class. (BJJ uses five different colors of belts to indicate the level of expertise: white, blue, purple, brown, and black.) We started with basic calisthenics to warm up. Afterward, we switched to jiu-jitsu–specific exercises: first, tumbling forward and backward to learn how to break our fall and then "shrimping" to learn how to escape an opponent. When you shrimp you lie on your side and push off the ground with a foot to drive your hips away from your opponent. While on your back (the bottom position), this creates distance from the dude on top, who wants to hold you tight. Hip movement is to BJJ what footwork is to boxing. "You've got good hips" is a common compliment in a BJJ gym, the only place on earth where you'll hear one man say that to another.

I made it through this first part of the class with only minor embarrassment. Despite my prodigious gut, I had bought a jiu-jitsu *gi* whose pants were at least two sizes too big. And so I had spent a great deal of time trying to keep my pants from falling down.

The next section was technique training and it involved the most awkward moment for any new kid at school: finding a partner. I felt like a transfer student. Almost everyone else already knew each other and paired up quickly. I stepped back against the wall and waited to see which unfortunate soul would find himself odd man out and thus be stuck with me.

A tall guy with Slavic features and blond hair drew the short straw. We shook hands and introduced ourselves as we watched Magno and a top student demonstrate the technique we were about to practice. My partner's name was Alexi, and he was from Ukraine but made sure to mention that he was actually Russian. He worked for Bank of America as an executive and had given up karate for jiu-jitsu, because, as he said, "I can't go to meetings with a black eye."

"I'm really sorry you got paired with me," I apologized, as we got ready to practice the hip toss we'd just seen demonstrated. "It's my first day."

He jumped back as if I just announced I had leprosy. Bruce Lee once said that the two types of fighters you never want to face are beginners and the insane, because you can't predict what they'll do. The scariest people at Renzo's were the first-day students, because they were the most likely either to go too hard and hurt you or, worse, make a stupid mistake and end up hurt by you. Everyone in a jiu-jitsu studio secretly believes in injury karma—what goes around comes around—and there was no worse karma than harming a beginner.

"Okay, we'll take this slow and easy today," Alexi said, as he gently grabbed my arm and waist. "We'll go fifty percent, yes?"

"Sounds good to me," I said, smiling inside.

(For the next three months, anytime I had a new training partner I always told him it was my first day.)

Being genuinely a first-day student, it didn't take long before I felt a sharp pain in my left thigh. Whenever you can feel pain while your body is already warm, you know it will be awful the next day.

"Ow!" I gasped.

"Sorry," he said. "Are you okay?"

"Fine, no worries, fine."

"Sorry," he said.

It was the most common exchange I'd hear over months of practice. Someone would gasp in pain and his training partner would apologize. No one wanted the bad karma.

Having finished the rather pro forma throwing section of the class—BJJ is almost exclusively interested in ground grappling with little concern for how the fight gets parallel to the earth—we moved to the heart of the style: position to submission. And the talk of position to submission in an overwhelmingly male sport inevitably involves a very common suspicion: There is something gay about BJJ, and by extension MMA.

While initially two men rolling around on the ground might

seem homoerotic, you have to watch only a few matches before you get past this. That is, unless you are an old boxer. Boxing's most prominent promoter, Bob Arum, said, "MMA is guys rolling around like homosexuals on the ground." Jay Larkin, who spent most of his career as a Showtime boxing executive, said, "To me, two guys rolling around on the floor is tedious, like watching gay foreplay."

But to be fair to the geezers, *Out* magazine sent a reporter to an MMA event to write an article titled "How Gay Is MMA?" (Their answer: very.) This is perhaps because every major jiu-jitsu position—with the exception of "side control," where the two bodies are perpendicular to each other like a lowercase t—has a corresponding name in the *Kama Sutra*. The guard is "missionary," the mount is "cowgirl," the rear mount is "doggy style," and north-south is "69."

When Magno told us to set up in the guard position, I had to hide an awkward smile as I rolled onto my back, spread my legs, waited for Alexi to crawl up to my crotch, and then wrapped my legs around his waist. But this smirk was quickly wiped away when Alexi jammed his right elbow into my gut and his left elbow hard into my thigh, breaking my leg lock around his waist ("opening the guard"). Then he dropped his knee onto the middle of my inner thigh. I gasped. He slid past to side control ("passing my guard"). Then he flipped a leg over my waist to secure mount. Panicked, I flipped over to my stomach. He hooked my legs with his feet and sunk into a choke hold. More specifically, a rear naked choke.

I tried to hold out as long as possible, but by squeezing my carotid artery he was lowering the blood pressure in my head. I felt dizzy, my vision blurred, and my body felt limp. I tapped out before my brain sounded the emergency alarm and started to shut down nonessential life functions (like consciousness). Alexi and I switched positions. While trying to pass his guard, I stuck my left arm underneath his leg. He grabbed my right arm, threw his leg over my head, locked it securely with his other leg, and squeezed. It's called a triangle choke, and I wish I could meet the evil genius who first thought it up, because it looks ridiculous and useless and yet I was tapping out within seconds.

Alexi had just proven to me Brazilian jiu-jitsu's paradigm shifting contribution to unarmed combat: You can win while lying flat on your back. In boxing and wrestling, it is considered the worst place to find yourself; in BJJ it is often where you want to be.

Magno gave us a moment to rest, relax, and chat before we started the third part of class: live rolling, which is the BJJ equivalent to sparring in boxing.

"Jiu-jitsu is incredibly complex," I said to Alexi. "With boxing, there are four basic punches: jab, cross, hook, and uppercut. Thai kickboxing has six punches, three elbows, two knees, and two basic kicks. But jiu-jitsu has hundreds of moves. It's like chess with blood."

"I wouldn't say chess," Alexi the Russian sniffed. "More like checkers."

It's actually more like chess, but I didn't want to insult the national pride of someone who was able to choke me out at will.

The coach called out for us to begin rolling.

There is nothing more exhausting than grappling. In striking martial arts styles, there are moments of separation and rest; in wrestling, it is an almost constant primal struggle of one person against the other, pushing and pulling. Professional boxing matches last thirty to forty-five minutes; Olympic wrestling matches max out at six.

Which is a roundabout way of saying that thirty minutes into the class I realized I had devolved into one of the lowest forms of creatures in a martial arts studio: the clock-watcher. Every few minutes, I'd crane my neck, hoping beyond hope that time had run out. I made it to the fifty-minute mark before I finally gave up, waving away Alexi and collapsing into the corner, my body deflated and my lungs screaming.

Bas Rutten, a first-rate Dutch kickboxer who made the switch to MMA and won a UFC heavyweight belt, told me the story of his first grappling class: "After it was over, I was driving home but was so tired I couldn't see clearly. I pulled over on the side of the highway, called my wife, and told her I'd give it three months but if it didn't get any easier I'd retire. Then I fell asleep for five hours."

My first post-class experience was more graphic. I made it to the subway platform before my stomach started to churn dangerously. I reached into a garbage can and pulled out a couple of empty Starbucks cups. I managed to squeeze onto the crowded train before everything inside me decided it was time to exit the front door. It was like a remake of *2 Girls 1 Cup*—but with one boy and two cups.

The experience did teach me an important NYC lesson. If you want a really good seat on a packed subway train, projectile vomiting is extremely effective. When I looked up from my heaving, I found myself completely alone on my side of the car with everyone else pressed against each other in the other half. It was like I had pulled out a gun.

I got home, collapsed into bed, and slept for twelve hours.

When I awoke, it felt like all the lactic acid in the universe was burning inside my left thigh. I had to push myself out of bed with my palms.

For ten days I hobbled nervously around Manhattan. You don't want to limp in the city. It's like being a wounded gazelle on the Serengeti. All the other predators look at you and think, *That guy can't make the rent.*

CHAPTER 4
Stockholm Syndrome

"A miserable childhood . . . was typically excellent
emotional preparation for what was required on a
football defense: it made you angry, it made you
aggressive, it made you want to tear someone's
head off. The NFL was loaded with players who
had mined a loveless, dysfunctional childhood . . ."

—MICHAEL LEWIS, *THE BLIND SIDE*

At Renzo's Academy—or, as I came to think of it, the University of Gracie New York (UGNY)—the main course of study was *gi* jiu-jitsu, that is, jiu-jitsu practiced while wearing a *gi*. The school's core course requirement was that students had to spend at least a year studying *gi* jiu-jitsu before being allowed to take any *gi*-free classes.

I found the emphasis odd. For an art form that is progressive in so many ways, *gi* jiu-jitsu represents an atypical attachment to tradition. The Gracies prefer *gi* because they believe it creates a more refined student, and also because that's what Mitsuyo Maeda wore when he taught the family in 1914. But in Brazil, *gi* versus no-*gi* has as much to do with class and racial divisions as it does with tradition. The Gracies were part of the whitish European elite: Carlos and Helio's grandfather, George, emigrated from Scotland; their father, Gastao, was a politician and businessman. The family and members of their class could afford to buy, maintain, and wash heavy *gi*s; poor kids from the favelas could not. And so from the underclass, a no-*gi* style arose called *luta livre* ("freestyle fighting").

In the grand tradition of the martial arts and young male pack psychology, students of the two different styles began feuding with each other. The pinnacle of the rivalry involved Renzo Gracie, who is very easygoing unless insulted. ("My name is not a bone to be carried in the jaw of a dog," he once said to a rival fighter, who had been bad-mouthing him, before slapping the guy and declaring, "You don't deserve my fist.") In 1997 he faced *luta livre* champion Eugenio Tadeu. The Rio de Janeiro crowd, filled with followers of both styles, rushed the cage and started spitting on the fighters. A *luta livre* fan climbed the fence and rained curses down on Renzo, who turned and broke the fan's nose, which caused a riot in the stadium and prematurely ended the competition.

Brazil's class rivalries were not my concern. MMA's rules do not allow fighters to wear a *gi* (only shorts), and I did not have time to spend an entire freshman year training *gi* jiu-jitsu. I needed to talk myself into the no-*gi* course of study. The problem was the no-*gi* classes were filled with senior students who were frighteningly good.

One day in the white belt *gi* class, I heard the guy next to me telling his friend about sneaking into one of the no-*gi* classes.

"How was it?" I asked.

"It wasn't so bad," he said, "if you don't mind being humiliated, dominated, and broken."

Days later I asked a more senior student what he thought of my switching to no-*gi*. "You're insane," he replied. "We call those classes the 'shark tank.' Even I won't take them, and I'm a purple belt."

The dean of the no-*gi* department at UGNY was a New Zealander named John Danaher, the only non-Brazilian on staff. Other than his broad back he wasn't that impressive to look at: average size and height, middle-aged, balding crown. To top it off, he had a gimpy left knee, which caused him to shuffle around the gym—back arched, butt out. The only indication that he was a martial artist was his fearsome expression. In the late afternoons, I'd often see him torturously stretching his legs. When he finished, he looked like he was ready to strangle puppies.

For weeks I tried screwing up the courage to approach him, but one look at his stark visage and I would chicken out. It wasn't until I saw him after one of his no-*gi* classes interacting with several of his students that I saw the other side. He was gently teasing them and his face was relaxed and his eyes warm. *He loves his students*, I thought. That was enough to prod me forward. I followed him into the back office.

After introducing myself and explaining my project, I asked him if I could join some of his classes.

"I know I'm not ready," I said. "But maybe you'd have some time for some private lessons to help me along."

"Of course." He smiled broadly.

In martial arts, like everywhere else, money talks. No coach in the city can earn enough to make rent teaching only general classes: They are essentially loss leaders that coaches use to gain private students. Private lesson fees also allow coaches to train pro fighters for free, which is crucial because pro fighters are always broke-ass. The pro fighters then serve as marketing tools for a coach, whose reputation depends on the quality of fighters he trains. The sport of MMA is subsidized by wannabe middle-class guys like me.

"You really talked a major publisher into paying you to study jiu-jitsu?" John asked, amused.

"Unfortunately."

"Oh, come on, that's the greatest job ever."

"Yeah, you're right," I relented. "It is a pretty awesome gig."

"Not to mention, you've already got a body like Fedor Eme-lianenko," he teased, referring to the world's best MMA fighter, who has a pear-shaped build. "So you're already halfway there."

"Actually, I look more like Roy 'Big Country' Nelson," I said. (Roy is so fat he actually uses his stomach as an offensive weapon, pinning it over his opponents' faces like he's trying to smother them with a pillow.)

John laughed and nodded. "Can you do Tuesday and Thursday at eleven?"

"Yeah," I said. "And, um, well, I was kinda just wondering: How much?"

"One hundred and fifty dollars."

"A lesson?"

"Yes."

I gulped. "Cash or check?"

"Cash is better. Strippers don't take checks."

■ ■ ■

Before my first private lesson, I attended John's general class to get a sense of what I was in for. It started when John walked in, slightly late, slipped off his shoes, and pointed to one of his students. He demonstrated a takedown, quickly and quietly.

I stood against the wall again, awkwardly, as longtime friends paired up with each other. One guy took mercy and offered to practice the move with me.

"It's my first day," I said.

"We'll take it easy," he said, assuringly.

The first half of John's hour-and-a-half-long class was spent learning individual techniques. His was a progressive approach. Each technique was linked to the next by a causal if-then pedagogy (a decision tree). If your opponent does this, then you do that. If your opponent does that, then you do this.

The second half was live sparring, or rolling. The goal was to test if you could actually apply the techniques learned in the first half of class against a training partner who was trying to use the same techniques to submit you. It is what gives BJJ its scientific aspect. You propose a certain technique as a hypothesis and then test it while rolling. If it works, you have a theory. If it doesn't, either you are doing it wrong or you need to discard it.

Live rolling was four six-minute rounds. My first partner was an engineering professor at City College. Immediately aware of how weak I was, he said, "I know I'm pretty heavy. I'll try to take it light on you."

A scrappy little fiftyish lawyer was my second. Given our size difference and his professional instincts, he didn't feel any need to take it light on me. As he was wrapping me up into knots and tying me up into a bow, I had the mental image of him sitting in some white-shoe law firm conference room, thinking to himself during the hours of frustrating negotiations, *Is counsel for the defense going to have to choke a bitch?*

Engineers, professors, lawyers, consultants, bankers. While jiu-jitsu attracts its fair share of young men with anger management problems, it is the first combat art in a long time to appeal to middle-aged white-collar professionals. And writers. What boxing was to Ernest Hemingway and Norman Mailer, jiu-jitsu has become to tough-guy writer-directors like John Milius, Guy Ritchie (who directed *Sherlock Holmes*), and David Mamet (who wrote and directed *Redbelt*, his pretentious cinematic take on the art).

This is in sharp contrast to Brazil, where jiu-jitsu is now considered in many circles a lowbrow, thuggish activity associated with "pit boys" (after pit bulls)—surfer gangs who terrorize the beaches. When I once congratulated Renzo on his new hometown of Holmdel, New Jersey, throwing him a Renzo Gracie Day parade, he replied, "Thank you, my friend. It is funny because my jiu-jitsu coach used to tell me that the only place the sport would take me was jail."

After the lawyer, I was such a wreck I tried to duck out early without John seeing me. However, before I got off the mat, Gary, a huge black guy, stabbed his finger into my chest. "You," he said simply. I'd seen him in the locker room several times after *gi* classes. He was a brown belt. I'd heard him talking about how many years he'd spent working for a black belt but he kept getting injured—his rotator cuff, MCL, etc.

Before I could blink, he jumped guard, throwing his legs around my waist and using his weight and his arms to pull me down on top of him. He immediately wrapped his right leg around my shoulder and stuck his foot under my chin as he used his immense arm strength to pull my head down. In short, he was using his instep to choke off my blood supply. It's called a *gogoplata* and considered to be a "low percentage" move in jiu-jitsu. I had no idea what he was doing, having never seen the move before, but I knew what it was like to be choked. Before I went to sleep, I tapped out.

When I researched the move later, I realized why he had picked me: He needed a warm, pliable body to try out a difficult technique. In a weird way, I felt a sense of relief. In the shark tank I had acquired a useful social function: I was the chum.

(Nearly six months later I saw Gary alone in the locker room on the day he received his black belt from Renzo. He just stood there holding and stroking it like, well, a big black belt. It was clearly one of the proudest moments of his life.)

My last training partner was a mid-fifties NYPD retiree. He immediately let me know that he was recently divorced. "Best thing about it is the bitch can't nag me no more why I'm always at the gym." In an unusual turn of events, I caught a second wind and suddenly had a feel for what I was doing. The cop kept trying to turn and twist me, and I was surprisingly able to resist his efforts. After we were done, he asked, "How long have you been practicing jiu-jitsu?"

"This is my first day."

He looked crushed.

When I later related this story to John, he burst out laughing. "There are only two true compliments in jiu-jitsu: How much do you weigh? And how long have you been training? Your first day . . . that must have killed him."

After class was over I sat against the wall, alternatively gulping in air and water. Chatting after class was nearly as an important part of the experience as rolling. I found myself falling into conversation with Brian. He had been a linebacker on Princeton's football team. After graduating from Penn law school, Brian had taken a job as a consultant for McKinsey.

"Someone is really paying you to write about MMA?" Brian asked incredulously. "God, I wish I had your job."

"I think yours pays a little better."

"Still."

"What I can't figure out how to do is explain in words just how complex jiu-jitsu is to the general public."

"Jiu-jitsu is so intricate," Brian suggested, helpfully, "that after every class I enter the new moves into an Excel document."

"Oh, that's perfect," I laughed. "Only a McKinsey consultant would think to generate BJJ spreadsheets."

■ ■ ■

John Danaher had a teasing, mocking, derisive sense of humor, which is funny so long as the barbs are pointed in a direction other than yours. The longer I knew him the more he reminded me of Hugh Laurie's character in *House*: crippled leg, brilliant mind, caustic wit with a dark view of human nature, intolerant of fools, and brutally honest.

"What are those?" were the first words he said to me during our first private lesson. He was pointing at the bright white volleyball knee pads I was wearing.

"Found these in storage. I think I wore them back in high school."

"They look like presidential knee pads," he ribbed. "They're your Monica Lewinsky knee pads."

"Well, Caol Uno wore pads just like these."

"Oh, that's a wonderful recommendation," John whooped.

(A champion grappler in Japan, Caol Uno got his ass and knee pads served to him when he came to the United States to fight in the UFC. The Japanese have had little success competing in America, which makes one wonder how fair the matches were at Japan's Pride FC events.)

"And what is happening with your shirt?" he continued.

I was wearing a bright yellow Nike with patented Dri-Fit technology. As far as advancements in human comfort are concerned, it is to a sweat-soaking cotton T-shirt what the Gillette Fusion is to the straight razor.

"I like this shirt."

John smiled before changing the subject. "So of all the topics to write about, why choose our outlaw sport?"

"It's the hottest in the country, and I have a background in martial arts. I used to fight in Chinese kickboxing matches."

"Did you?" John asked, and then paused for a moment. "When I was at university, my philosophy professor told me that anytime a young man decided to major in philosophy he always wondered, 'What's wrong with you?' I feel the same way when somebody wants to become a fighter: 'What's wrong with you?'"

"Unfortunately, it was only the bullies who beat me up when I was a kid," I said. "That's why I was good at martial arts but never great. Now if it had been my father . . ."

"And if only your uncle had stuck his thumb up your bum," John laughed, "you might be a world champion."

"I can't tell from your accent: Australia or New Zealand?"

"Do I look like someone whose ancestors were British thieves and tax cheats?"

"Ah, so you're a Velcro-gloved, sheep-fucking New Zealander."

"Indeed."

"Ever think about going back?"

"When a convict escapes from prison, does he return voluntarily?"

"Renzo told me you were a philosophy professor at Columbia."

"He likes to exaggerate," John said. "I was a Ph.D. candidate there. However, I never finished my thesis. I still could, but I don't see the economic upside."

"What was it about?"

"The title was 'Rationality Conditions for Theory Change in the Physical Sciences.'"

Digging deep down into my faltering long-term memory, I took a stab at it, "Like Cone?"

"Kuhn," John replied, rolling his eyes.

"Ah, Kuhn, right. As you can see, I never got past the master's stage in philosophy," I said. "By the way, how did a philosophy grad student get into jiu-jitsu?"

"When I came here, I didn't have much money, and I quickly blew my first stipend on wine and women. I realized I'd be bankrupt before the next semester check arrived. I didn't want to be a waiter because they spend their lives being ordered around like servants. To be a bartender you needed to have connections. So I ended up working as a bouncer. I was already good at fighting. But I was shocked to discover that the best American bouncers were former collegiate wrestlers. We didn't have amateur wrestling in New Zealand. To improve as a bouncer I knew I needed to study wrestling. Somewhere I read an ad for something that was called 'Brazilian ground fighting.' I had heard that these Brazilians were fearless fighters, and their style had more in common with street fighting than amateur wresting.

"Now the next question you're going to ask me is," John continued, "why did I continue bouncing after I had the connections to become a bartender?"

Actually my next question was: What NYC nightclub hires an average-size white guy with a limp? Every club I'd been in, the bouncers looked like aspiring NFL linebackers. But I decided discretion was the better part of valor. If Manhattan clubs had repeatedly hired him, John had to be an extra level of scary.

"Bartenders are constantly busy, and I needed time to study. Bouncing is like what George Orwell said about war: 'It's ninety-nine percent boredom and one percent sheer terror,'" John said with a flicker in his eyes. "During the ninety-nine percent, I studied philosophy and prepared for classes that I was teaching."

"But you enjoyed the one percent as well."

"As is every man's God-given right. Now, let's get you started, young man."

Like his general class, John didn't waste time with warm-ups or stretching—it was straight to technique, only in private he was my training partner. It was "one-for-one," which meant he'd show the move on me, then I'd attempt it on him, then he'd reshow it on me, then I'd attempt it again until either I finally got it right or I had so annoyed him that he decided to move on.

"In jiu-jitsu, we don't deal in problems," John said with emphasis. "We deal in dilemmas. Problems can be solved. Dilemmas force a choice between two bad outcomes."

His example was taking an opponent's back. John sat behind me with his legs and arms wrapped around my torso. His first and best attacking option was a rear naked choke (sleeper hold). If I didn't defend by tucking in my chin and grabbing his arm, he'd quickly sink in the choke and I'd either tap out or pass out. But if I did defend, he could easily grab an arm, throw a leg over my head, and put me in an arm bar, where he could snap my elbow if I didn't tap.

"You see? No good outcomes," he said.

"Heads you win, tails I lose," I replied.

"Exactly. In your training, I'm going to focus on your bottom defense, because you won't be on top much," John told me. "The MMA guys you're going to fight will, unlike you, probably have a wrestling background. They will also be younger, stronger, faster, better conditioned, and more experienced."

"Will I have any advantages?"

"Well, hopefully you'll be smarter."

Having John on top of me was like having a car parked on my chest. Given his weight (probably fifty pounds less than mine), he shouldn't have felt that heavy, but he did. John called it the difference between subjective and objective weight. He ascribed it to physics and biomechanics: knowing where and how to use force and pressure. He had me tapping out not from any submission hold but simply from the pressure on my chest.

"Why are you thrashing about?" John asked.

"Because I can't breathe," I gasped.

"That's a good reason," he laughed. "We call that drowning man syndrome. It is when someone essentially drowns himself. He has the ability to escape and save himself, but because he panics and thrashes about, he tires himself out. He defeats himself without his opponent having to do any of the hard work of securing a submission. You need to learn how to move your hips."

As he worked techniques on top of me, I tried to shrimp out like I'd learned in my other classes—pushing my hips out and away from him so our bodies were at an angle and my back was not flat on the mat. Bottom defense was all about achieving separation from your opponent on top.

It took less than ten minutes for the warning light on my gas gauge to flash. When I was eighteen I would have given 110 percent and kept going until my tank ran empty. At thirty-six, I'd reached the point where eighty-five to ninety percent was more than enough. Better to feign weakness and keep the reserves hidden.

"Your problem is that you're too tense," John admonished me. "You flop around like a fish. It wastes energy. It's not efficient. Look at me. If you saw me in a sports club you wouldn't be impressed. I had a marathoner come train with me last week. Presumably his cardio is pretty good. He lasted fifteen minutes. I can roll for eight hours a day. I'm not in better shape; I'm more efficient."

"Okay."

"Look, I'm crippled," John said, bringing up the elephant in the room.

"Um, yeah, I, ah, noticed."

"Of course you did," John laughed. "Either that or I've got a dildo up my arse."

"How did it happen?" I asked, assuming it was a jiu-jitsu–related injury.

"Since I was little. Must have been all those nuclear tests in the

South Pacific," he half-heartedly joked. "I guess my father's webbed feet should have been a clue."

It was a dodge, but I didn't press. Bullies had beaten the crap out of me simply for being a bookish kid, and I didn't have a bum knee. They must have been hell on him. But amazingly he had found the one martial art that is done almost exclusively lying down—until someone invents Barcalounger fu.

"Remember, you need to learn how to be more efficient," John said, repeating himself, "because the guys you'll be fighting will be younger, stronger, faster, and more skilled than you."

"But I'll be smarter."

"Maybe," he said, standing up. "I need to make a call. We'll roll after."

After he'd left, the words *stronger, faster,* and *more skilled* kept spinning around and around in my head like a washing machine. As they cycled faster and faster, I could feel Pride rear its ugly head.

"He's calling you a pussy," Pride said, fucking with me.

"No, he's making a statement of fact," I reasoned. "They will be younger, stronger, faster, and more experienced than me."

"He keeps repeating it," Pride replied. "Why? Cause he thinks you're a pussy."

"He's just trying to mentally prepare me for how tough this will be for me."

"You once fought the national champion of China," Pride said, puffing up.

"That was a long time ago."

"You need to show him you're not a pussy."

When John came back, he lay down on his back, perpendicular to me. He was giving me side mount. It would be like in tennis if he let me start each game up thirty-love. John does this with all of his students, but I didn't know this at the time.

"See, this asshole thinks you're a pussy," Pride said. "Show him you're not."

Usually training partners start slowly to establish a rhythm, but my pride was wounded. As soon as we slapped hands to begin, I dove at him, squeezing him as hard as I could, digging my shoulder into his chest. I had no idea what I was doing, but I was going to make damn sure he knew I wasn't a pussy.

After a moment of surprise, John shrimped out, spun me back into guard, reversed me, and locked in an arm bar. It took no more than five seconds for him to tap me out.

If anything, this made me more furious. Like a wounded bull I kept charging, and he kept spinning out of the way and bleeding me as I went by. It happened so fast that I can no longer remember the order of the submissions, but they ran the gamut from arm locks to triangles to rear naked chokes. At a certain point his dominance was so absurdly complete that the rage flushed out of me. I started laughing.

"John, if you tap me out ten times in less than a minute, do I get the eleventh one for free?"

Still keyed up and in the zone, John simply shook his head and submitted me a few more times, before taking mercy.

"That was interesting," John said as he rolled to his knees.

"I strangely enjoyed it."

"Did you know a skilled torturer is able to make his victims empathize with him?" John asked.

"Yeah," I said. "It's called Stockholm syndrome."

"You know what you should do?" John laughed. "Call my chapter 'Stockholm Syndrome.'"

■ ■ ■

"What was John like?" Em asked me as I dragged my broken self into the apartment.

"Fascinating. Complicated. He's crazy smart with this dark, caustic wit. He comes off as a curmudgeon, but it hides a big heart. He clearly loves his students. His skills are freaky good. I attacked him with everything I had; it was like there was a force field around him. No way to best him. And he has this crippled knee, so he walks like he needs a cane or a walking stick."

"Sounds like you're training with Yoda."

"What did you say?"

"Why are you smiling at me like that?"

"Say that again."

"What?"

"Yoda."

"Stay away. What are you doing? Let . . . go . . . of . . . me! Don't kiss me!"

"Come on, baby, make another *Star Wars* reference."

"What is your leg doing?"

"It's jiu-jitsu," I said. "I'm controlling your hips."

"You let my hips go!"

"Say 'Yoda' one more time."

"I'll die first!"

That evening John texted: "For our second class we can examine some other aspect of BJJ and increase the set of skills that you currently possess and bring it closer to the set of skills that you OUGHT to possess."

"Looking forward to moving from 'is' to 'ought,'" I tapped back.

Replying immediately, he wrote: "The chasm from 'is' to 'ought' is indeed a wide one in the realm of moral philosophy . . . wider still in the realm of jiu-jitsu . . . but where there is a (non-Kantian) will . . ."

And because I can't stand not to get the last word in, I replied, ". . . there is a (Nietzschean) way."

When I proudly showed this exchange to Em, she just shook her head.

"How did you two nerds ever find each other?"

CHAPTER 5
The Monster Mash

"Jesus Didn't Tap"

—NAME OF A CHRISTIAN MMA CLOTHING COMPANY

The most pleasurable part of John's private classes were the five-to ten-minute bull sessions before and after. A polymath with a near photo-perfect memory, John could fluently cover almost any topic.

For comedy, he could quote verbatim sections of *Blackadder*. ("Sir, you are one of the most foul, disgusting, immoral, perverted men that I have ever known. Have you considered a career in the church?") For philosophy, he'd come up with random anecdotes to illustrate jiu-jitsu principles. (When I suggested that a particular move was too complicated, he said, "You want to know complicated? Heidegger used to give lectures so purposely obscure that at the end of lecture he'd ask the class if anyone understood him. If one person raised their hand he'd furiously wipe off the chalkboard and start over again until no one knew what he was saying.") For history, he would focus on anything war-related, from Genghis Khan to World War II. (He liked to joke that my new diet and workout regimen was the Battle of the Bulge.)

By far John's favorite topic of discussion was his favorite student, Georges St-Pierre, the UFC welterweight champion better known by fans as GSP, although he dislikes the nickname and all his close friends call him Georges. John loved all his students, but he had a mythic place in his heart for GSP. And what coach wouldn't? The French Canadian fighter is a once-in-a-lifetime student. Not only is he widely considered one of the top pound-for-pound fighters in the sport, but he is also humble, thoughtful, and unfailingly polite. He is the gentleman warrior.

"The first time Georges came to Renzo's, he was an unknown fighter in the Canadian promotions," John told me. "He came to my beginner class and did well with the other blue belts, but then he rolled with my friend Shawn, who is very talented."

"How'd it go?" I asked.

"Not so well for him." John smiled. "After it was over, I saw him in the corner with his hands in his face. It looked like he was in tears. I went over to make sure he wasn't hurt. He couldn't speak English back then, so his girlfriend of the time told me that Georges was so humiliated that he felt like quitting the sport."

"I sympathize," I said. "Are you training GSP for his fight against Serra?"

Matt Serra was one of Renzo's most senior and most successful pupils. Because much of the top MMA talent is concentrated in a small number of gyms, fighters from the same schools occasionally find themselves pitted against each other, dividing loyalties among teammates and coaches. Serra had beaten GSP a year previously, and the rematch was hotly anticipated because most MMA fans felt that GSP was the superior fighter and that Serra had won with a lucky punch.

"That's been difficult," John said, looking genuinely pained. "Matt is Renzo's senior student, the school's first American black belt. I was one of his students, and we train together before his fights. On the other hand, Georges is my student."

"You could train them both."

"No. After Georges lost to Matt Serra he said some things that made Matt angry, so Matt and Renzo had Georges banned from the school."

"I've never heard of anything like that," I said, surprised. "I can understand why he'd be pissed if GSP was making excuses, trying to take away from his victory, but to ban him . . ."

"It's awkward." John smiled, sadly.

■ ■ ■

When John was in a good mood, he was an utter delight. When in a bad one, he could be terrifying. Sometimes I could change his disposition by asking him a question that caught his interest. Before every class I mentally prepared a list of questions in case of emergency.

On one of those dark days when nothing I did was right and John was getting more and more annoyed, I asked him what he thought of B.J. Penn's high guard, where he locks his legs high on his opponent's shoulders to prevent them from striking.

Like the flip of a switch, John brightened and became extremely animated.

"Everyone talks about B.J. Penn's bottom defense. Don't get me wrong. He's a world-class jiu-jitsu player, one of the top ten best ever, but he doesn't win fights from the bottom. He wins with his guard-passing skill, mount control, and uncanny ability to stand back up from bottom position," John said. "Here's your assignment for next week. Go home and find me one match that B.J. Penn won from the bottom. Just one."

(I did go home and look it up, but I knew I didn't need to. John doesn't give assignments where he doesn't already know the answer.)

"Here," John continued. "Put me into the high guard. I'll show you how to counter it. This is what I taught Georges when I was preparing him for B.J. Penn."

I wrapped one leg high on his back and grabbed my ankle with my opposite hand and hugged him close. John shoved both fists through so that his forearms were resting on my chest, and then he did a push-up as he bridged his back, breaking the hold. Then he surprised me by throwing a right elbow strike aimed at my face.

Time slowed down like in a car accident, everything became vivid, and I swear it looked like John doubled in size. Bruce Banner had turned into the Hulk.

As I looked into John's eyes, I saw his monster behind them. And it was huge.

Stopping his elbow just millimeters away from my nose, John sat back and said, "You see, like any hold, high guard can be countered. There's no way to maintain it if you just push straight back. And once the hold is broken, you are wide open to elbows, punches."

John continued speaking, with a professional's pride in his work. But I couldn't hear a word he was saying because the monster behind my eyes—terrified at seeing another monster so much bigger—was screaming bloody murder in my head.

"Kill him! Kill him! Kill him! Get a knife! Get a gun! Kill him!"

Now, now, I thought, trying to placate my monster. *John's a good guy. He's our teacher. He was just showing us a move.*

John continued to talk and I continued to pretend to listen as the argument with the monster raged in my head. Finally, John slapped my leg to get my attention.

"Concentrate," John said, angrily. "You're as tense as a virgin on prom night. What's wrong with you?"

His question posed something of a moral dilemma. On the one hand, you never should lie to your martial arts instructor, but on the other, you don't want to tell him that your mind wandered because the monster inside you was plotting his gruesome murder. It tends to lead to awkward silences. And I hate those.

"I'm sorry, John."

"Relax. You're always so tense," he said. "You should smoke some dope before class."

"You want me to toke up like all the Brazilians?" I asked.

"No, no, I'm not saying that. I'm just joking, sort of."

I never took up the spliff because I already have enough munchies, giggles, and paranoia in my life without chemical enhancement. But it was probably to my disadvantage. For the first few months I was so stressed and inwardly turned that when John and I would roll I'd inadvertently talk out loud to myself.

The first time, I said, "That was stupid, Matthew!"

The outburst so surprised John that he started laughing and let go of the triangle choke he had me in.

"Yes, Matthew," John said, as he reapplied the choke. "It was."

The second time was when he had caught me in an arm bar.

"No, I don't want this," I said to myself.

"We don't always get what we want," John replied.

The third time was when John trapped me in a variation of a move aptly named the crucifix. He had twisted me around so I was lying perpendicular to him with my back on his stomach. My left arm was trapped and spread wide by his legs. My right arm was trapped and spread wide under his armpit. My head was being yanked to the right with his hands. John arched his back, stretching me on the rack.

"I don't know how I got into this position," I cried out. "All I wanted was to be a writer."

John laughed so hard he nearly lost the hold, but then he righted himself and cranked my neck toward him.

"I invented this variation," he whispered in my ear.

■ ■ ■

Another favorite way we passed the time before and after private lessons was to make fun of Matt Hughes, who was formerly the dominant welterweight (170 pounds) in the UFC and by all accounts a first-rate prick. For John, the pleasure came from the fact that his friends Georges St-Pierre and Matt Serra were also welterweights and fervent rivals of Matt Hughes, so John spent a great deal of his time and mental energy thinking of strategies to beat Hughes. For me, it was because Matt Hughes reminded me of all those asshole wrestlers I grew up with in Kansas who used to shove me into the lockers.

Our other favorite target of derision was the recent burst of MMA memoirs, which had replaced the pro wrestling autobiographies as the hot new trend in book publishing (just as MMA had largely taken pro wrestling's spot in popular culture). So when John and I found out that Matt Hughes was coming out with his own autobiography, *Made in America*, it was like Christmas morning.

"Have you read it?" John asked, excitedly, just days after it hit the stands.

"I haven't picked up a copy yet," I apologized.

"You must, you must," John insisted. "That's your assignment for next week."

When next week arrived, John grinned widely as I sat down for our pre-class chat.

"So what did you think?"

"Holy shit," I said. "Was there anyone he didn't stab in the back? I mean the things he said about Tim Sylvia . . ."

"It was like low-rent Machiavelli," John said. "I felt dirty after reading it. I wanted to take a shower."

"You know the only person he didn't harsh was his coach, Pat Miletich."

"Which means Pat must be a saint on the level of Mother Teresa," John laughed. "His Iowa school seems less and less like a fight gym and more like a halfway house for troubled youth."

"I can't believe the UFC let him publish this screed," I said. "UFC contracts are so restrictive, a fighter pretty much gives up everything but his first-born son. Why not publishing rights? At the very least they could have a decent ghostwriter on staff."

"Or an editor to cut out the boob job sex scenes," John laughed.

"No, no, no, please don't bring that up."

"You have a copy of the book with you?" John asked. "Give it to me."

"Oh, this is gonna hurt worse than Tito Ortiz's memoir."

Immediately flipping to the exact page, John read out loud:

I leaned further and kissed her, being very careful that my hands didn't brush up and hurt her. In fighting, you always want to be on your back. But sometimes it's good in other situations too. I barely felt her weight as I eased her on top of me. As we moved together on my bed her stitches ripped a little bit and her blood drizzled across my chest. I lived in a world where people were bound by their blood, rolling in practice rooms and cages. It was the first time I'd had that kind of bond on the bedsheets. We were together again, and it felt wonderful.

"I may never be able to masturbate again," I said.

"But that wasn't as disturbing to me as when his twin brother and friends converted him to Christianity," John said. "It was like he was abducted by a cult."

"What I don't get is why all these hard-core fighters, like Hughes and Franklin, choose Jesus as their deity. He had a lot of wonderful things to say, but he wasn't much of a warrior."

"He definitely had a losing record against the Romans," John laughed.

"You'd think they'd pick a more militaristic god," I said. "Like Ares."

"Or Thor."

"But at least you can say this about our Lord and Savior," I said. "Jesus didn't tap."

■ ■ ■

Just as I was told when I first arrived, it was nearly six months to the day that everything finally clicked. It was like learning a foreign language. After hours and hours of memorizing vocabulary and grammar, I suddenly was capable of holding a rudimentary conversation. When John pushed, I pulled; when he pulled, I pushed. Instead of thrashing around desperately, I flowed, sliding

easily from position to position, escaping locks and slipping submissions. I was in the zone, not overthinking everything, not con-
sciously thinking at all. It took several minutes before I realized
what I was doing.

John sat back on his heels and looked at me with surprise and
no small amount of pride in his work.

"Your composure has shot through the roof," John said.

But before I could start purring, he smirked. "Of course, compared to before, that's not saying much. You used to flop around
like a drunk cockroach."

"I know, I know."

"So, for the next chapters of your book, are you planning to
train with Pat Miletich in Iowa or one of the other camps?"

"I think I'll stick around for another six months," I said. "I'm
still so bad I don't want to shame you by going somewhere else and
telling them that you were my teacher."

"Yes, we need you to sign a nondisclosure agreement," John
laughed. "From here on, you must refer to me as Bob Danaher."

"Agreed," I said. "So, Bob, I am going to continue training
with you, but I will be gone for the next two weeks. I'm traveling
to Bangkok to study Thai kickboxing."

(The UFC was created to prove that Gracie jiu-jitsu was the
best martial art. But as the sport evolved in the petri dish of the
Octagon, it slowly became obvious that the ultimate MMA fighter
needed the best elements from four different combat styles: the
punches, footwork, and head movement of Western boxing; the
kicks, knees, and elbows of Thai kickboxing; the takedowns, takedown defenses, and ground control of American collegiate wrestling; and the submissions of Brazilian jiu-jitsu. *Cross-training*
became the biggest buzzword in MMA, and *one-dimensional* the

biggest insult. Renzo was one of the first Gracies to add a Thai kickboxing dimension to his toolbox.)

"When you get back," John said, "we need to find you a Muay Thai instructor here."

"Who do you suggest?"

"I sent Georges to study with Phil Nurse at his gym in Chinatown."

"That's the highest recommendation you could give."

"Let's stop on a high note, young man," John said. "I'll see you when you return."

ACT II

MUAY THAI AND SAMBO

CHAPTER 6
Bangkok Vice

"If he can't walk, he can't fight. If he can't breathe,
he can't fight. If he can't think, he can't fight."

—TRADITIONAL MUAY THAI SAYING

A Marine, a fisherman, and a writer walk into a ping-pong show.

The setup for this joke started at Rajadamnern Stadium in Bangkok, Thailand. Along with Lumpini Stadium, this is where Thai men go to drink, gamble, and watch Thai boys punch, kick, knee, and elbow one another in what is one of the most brutal sports on earth: Thai kickboxing (Muay Thai). As a student of all things martial arts–related, I found myself sitting in the Western (*farang*) section next to a Marine, who was wiry, intense, and twenty years old, and an Alaskan fisherman, a strapping lad with the kind of fresh-faced awkwardness I associate with the home-schooled.

We kept our conversation focused on the fights themselves

until the Marine surprised me by asking, "Have you read the Patriot Act?"

"No, I've read about it," I said. "I didn't think anyone had read it, not even the politicians who signed it into law."

"Well, I've spent some time studying the document, and I find it frightening how easily they can take away our rights."

"And you're a Marine on R&R from Iraq?" I blurted out.

"Why?" he shot back, mistakenly thinking I was questioning his right to R&R. "It's my final tour of duty."

"Your second or your third?"

"Oh, you've been paying attention," he said, smiling in such a grateful way, as if surprised that anyone back home cared, that it made my stomach clench with guilt. "It's my third. I'll be done in May."

Before I could stop myself, I made the sign of the cross.

The thought of going home sent the Marine into a reverie about what he would do when his tour of duty was up. He wanted to make some real money, maybe do something in engineering. He'd never been as good at school as his sister, who, he proudly told us, was at Harvard, but he'd always liked math.

"But only if I come back in one piece. If not, I've got my Disfigured and Disabled List," he said. When it was clear we didn't understand, he continued. "If I come back all fucked up, it's the list of people whom I'm going to sort out."

Muay Thai is the national sport, but only for Thai men. Thai women detest it—several I met called me a "bad boy" for expressing an interest in it—for the simple reason that after a night spent drinking, gambling, and learning new ways to hurt someone, their men either come home drunk, broke, and angry or they don't come home at all. *Butterfly* is the Thai term for men who want to pollinate every flower.

The beers had worked enough Dr. Jekyll/Mr. Hyde magic that we all knew we weren't going home yet.

"Pat Pong?" the Marine asked rhetorically.

"Yeah," I said, knowing I shouldn't. My first Muay Thai class was scheduled for the next day, and the dumbest thing I could do was show up for the hardest sport on earth tired and hungover. But the irony was too perfect to pass up. Pat Pong, Bangkok's garish red-light district, had been built for U.S. soldiers on R&R leaves from Vietnam—the last time we tried to manage a civil war in Asia.

The *tuk-tuk* driver took one look at the state of us and asked, "Pat Pong? Ping-pong show?"

We still had enough of our wits about us to recognize with one look at the bar (no windows) and the neighborhood he dropped us off in (quiet, residential) that we'd been had. In our infinite wisdom, we decided to walk to Pat Pong.

It took an hour and six 7-Eleven stops for directions, beer, cigarettes, and a bottle of Johnnie Walker Red before we wandered into Pat Pong, a flea market bazaar that turns into a bizarre market for sex at night. Touts, *tuk-tuk* drivers, and flirty bar girls line the streets trying to entice *farang*, the drunker the better, into various establishments.

As we made arrangements with a tout to take us in, I waved away the Marine as he reached into his pocket. Having done little for the war effort other than shop, I figured the least I could do was buy a Marine a fifty-dollar ping-pong show.

As he thanked me, he seemed so young and vulnerable that it

called to mind something my father had said to me before I left: "Before I put your mother on the phone, I want to talk to you about your trip to Bangkok. I know from my time over there that the Thai women, well, they are even more beautiful than the women of Rio. They are so, ah, delicate. But with all the prostitution, the venereal diseases, they are fireships."

I was so stunned—because he so rarely speaks about his service in Vietnam, and he had never before used an adjective like *delicate* in reference to women with me—that I failed to ask him what he meant and had to go online to find out the definition of *fireships*.

"Do you know what a fireship is?" I asked the Marine.

"Sure, a fireship was a boat filled with explosives, set on fire, and set into an enemy fleet back when ships were made of wood. Why?"

As I stared at him with concern, a flicker of annoyance crossed his visage. "This isn't my first time in Bangkok."

So a Marine, a fisherman, and a writer walk into a ping-pong show.

It was a black box with an elongated stage in the center, surrounded on three sides by a bar, with seating up front and a second elevated level against the walls. As soon as we entered, we were surrounded by waitresses, working girls, and "masseuses." By the time drinks were ordered and we were seated at the bar, I realized the Marine had disappeared.

Twenty minutes later, I looked around and realized the fisherman had disappeared as well. I found myself sitting next to a lovely young woman from Cambridge and her Scottish boyfriend— surprisingly enough, half the audience was *farang* women.

On stage, five absolutely stunning Thai women in bikinis danced listlessly, while at regular intervals a naked, chubby Thai woman entered, dropped to her knees, and proceeded to pull various household items out of her moneymaker—the more dangerous-seeming, the better. The first time, she grabbed a string, and out came two dozen one-inch nails. The next performance was razor blades. Watching it felt like undergoing FBI profiling: If you find this erotic, you may be a serial killer.

The only nonmacabre moment was the mini bananas (ping-pong balls are apparently out of fashion and were never used), which the performer would individually chamber and then catapult into the crowd. As we ducked the incoming missiles, I realized too late that the front row was the splash zone. It was like *The Vagina Monologues* meets the Shamu show at SeaWorld.

By the time the fisherman returned with a very happy-looking Thai woman under each arm, I had grown bored with the show itself but rather entranced with one of the stunning dancers in the back. It was the Cambridge woman who delivered the *Crying Game* surprise: "The dancers? They are all ladyboys."

"No!" I exclaimed, jumping out of my seat, taking a closer look and feeling very much like a boy from Kansas. "Damn!"

One of the perennial questions about Thailand is why ladyboys (*kathoey*) are so much more accepted and such a bigger part of the culture than anywhere else on the planet. In *Bangkok 8*, which is by far the most entertaining book ever written about Thailand, Buddhism is offered as the answer; specifically, the idea that since each soul has gone through multiple reincarnations as both a male and a female, gender distinction is blurrier than in other faiths.

Maybe. My personal theory is that if your country's major source of revenue is tourism, and sexual tourism is a significant portion of that, then you'd want to offer every item on the menu. The latest trend is Japanese women and Thai go-go boys.

In the middle of this deep thought, the madam of the house, a tiny, wizened old crone, rushed up to me and grabbed my arm in terror, "You friend! You friend! He no get up!"

"He can't get it up?" I asked very confused. "What am I supposed to do about that?"

"No! He no get up! He no wake! No can wake you friend!"

"Where is he?" I asked, trying not to panic.

In the bathroom, she opened a side door and led me into the establishment's brothel: a hallway and five tiny rooms. In the third was the Marine, lying flat on his back and naked as the day he was born. For decorum's sake, someone had thoughtfully thrown a washcloth over his privates. Quickly surveying the room, I saw his clothes on the floor and with some relief noted an opened condom wrapper. He had been in Bangkok before.

The relief vanished as I shook his shoulder and he didn't move. I shook him harder, and still he didn't move.

Stepping back, my first thought was: *My God, I let one of our boys die on my watch*. This was followed by a second more horrifying thought: *What am I going to tell his mother?*

Panicked, I shouted at him, "Get up!"

He remained dead to the world.

I leaned near his ear and shouted in my best *Full Metal Jacket* drill-sergeant impression, "Marine! On your feet, maggot!"

Like a coiled spring, he was up and standing at attention.

"I think it's time for us to go," I said, handing him his jeans. "I'll wait for you outside."

As I was trying to explain to the fisherman why we should make our exit, the Marine came barreling out of the bathroom. His eyes were wild, still half-stuck in a drunken nightmare. He grabbed my arm and whispered, "We gotta get the fuck outta here." And then he tore down the stairs at full speed.

By the time I had rounded up the troops and made it to the street, he was long gone. "Should we look for him?" I asked.

"If he can survive Fallujah," the fisherman said, "he can survive Bangkok."

"Just to be safe."

As we searched Pat Pong, I thought about how politicians are always calling the troops the greatest soldiers in history, and it struck me that while deifying was better than demonizing them, it still lessened their humanity and thus made their suffering more mythical and less real and thus less guilt-inducing.

Was this Marine part of the greatest warrior culture in history? I don't know. The blockbuster *300* had made a pretty good case for the Spartans. What I do know is that anyone who reads the Patriot Act and worries over its consequences is far better than we deserve. My biggest hope is he returned in one piece.

■ ■ ■

Standing unsteadily in front of my hotel the next morning, I waited for a taxi to take me to my lesson. The bellhop stared at my pale, sweaty face and asked, "You really want to make Muay Thai today?"

"No," I replied.

Bangkok has the feel of São Paulo and the traffic of Los Angeles. It was a long ride in stop-and-go gridlock.

"You like Muay Thai?" my driver, a pleasant middle-aged woman, asked me.

"Yes," I said. "Do you?"

"Not so much."

Windy Sport Boxing Gym, located in the shadow of Lumpini Stadium, was a converted open-air garage with all the sweat, dedication, and poor-boy desperation of classic boxing gyms of yore. It had a ring, punching bags, and padded equipment strewn across the floor. As I was changing in the back, I noticed three students taking a siesta in a side room. It was two in the afternoon. Given the muscle-sapping heat of Thailand, Muay Thai boxers practice early in the morning and late in the afternoon, sleeping the humid midday hours away.

My instructor was Peter, a twenty-two-year-old from the north. He would rather have been napping but was up for me to help pay the rent. I didn't mind. I was there to help pay mine.

We started with the basics, which are always the hardest to learn. Muay Thai fighters stand with their hands high and their elbows out to create a cage around their head. When elbow strikes are an option, you'd much rather create an impenetrable defense around your skull and leave your cage open than the other way around.

It took all of ten minutes—okay, it was five—before I was gasping for breath and Peter was sitting me down and handing me a bottle of water.

"Bangkok is hot," he said, trying to sound sympathetic.

The key to Muay Thai is shin kicks, delivered in roundhouses to the legs, ribs, and head. Muay Thai fighters start training in year-round camps at the age of ten or eleven. Many start their professional careers at thirteen. If they are lucky, they will make it to twenty-five. To turn their shins into weapons, they spend hours beating them with wooden staffs to calcify the bone. Peter's shins looked like they had barnacles beneath the skin.

"Muay Thai is not karate. Drive through the body," Peter said, as we practiced the full commitment of a Muay Thai roundhouse.

When I was a boy, we used to have a game where two of us would exchange punches to the arm until one of us quit. This is Muay Thai, only with kicks, punches, knees, and elbows.

The previous night, at the fights at Rajadamnern Stadium, I'd seen the most amazing thing. In the third round of the fifth fight, each fighter had locked his arms around the other's head, and they exchanged brutal knees to each other's chests. Back and forth it went until the bell rang, ending the round. I assumed that was it, and they would return to fighting strategically, looking for advantages to win decisively. But when the bell for round four rang, they ran toward each other, locked up, and spent the next three minutes exchanging knees, one-for-one. In round five, they did the same. I've never seen anything like it. Their chests were pulped like raw meat, but neither seemed to care. It was a test of fortitude to see who could remain standing.

There is a ritualistic dance before each fight that many foreign writers have seized upon to indicate that Muay Thai is more than a gladiatorial sport. But the truth is, human sacrifice has always been a religious spectacle. Boxing gloves weren't added until the twentieth century. In the past, Muay Thai fighters would wrap their hands in cloth, dip the cloth into resin, and then roll their resin-wrapped hands into a pile of broken glass (as in the movie *Kickboxer*). Death was the common end result.

As John Keegan explains in *A History of Warfare*, these fights were often used to settle disputes between tribes, especially with the Burmese. It was the single-combat model, like Achilles versus Hector or David versus Goliath. It was brutal, but it was better than the alternative—total war.

When we reached the light sparring phase of the lesson, I led with my best technique. I tapped him in the chest with a side kick and then put the same kick onto the tip of his nose. My eyes lit up with surprise at his lack of defensive skills, until it dawned on me (much later and after much pain) that he wasn't worried about defense, because there was no way I could hurt him. His eyes lit up because he realized I was just barely good enough that he could play with me. He ducked his head behind his arms and entered with a roundhouse kick to the thigh, a jab to the face, a knee to the chest, and an elbow to the temple.

Fortunately, he held back on all those attacks, which is why I am still on this earth and able to write this book. I bowed, and he bowed back. The sacrificial act was pantomimed but not completed.

As the lesson came to an end, the rest of his students gathered around me. Feeling awkward, I tried for a moment of cross-cultural exchange.

"Tony Jaa," I said, referring to the Thai kickboxing film star who had recently become Thailand's answer to Bruce Lee.

Not understanding the Anglicized version of the actor's name, they looked at me with confusion.

"*Ong-bak*," I said, referring to the flick that made Tony Jaa famous in international martial arts movie circles.

"Ah, *Ong-bak*!" they all cried.

Peter then proceeded to teach me all the wild moves that Tony Jaa used in his movies: flying knees, double elbows, spinning shin kicks.

It was awesome.

CHAPTER 7
Nursery School

"Honest effort and sterling character backed by
solid instruction will carry a man a good way, but
unearned natural ability has a lot to be said for it."

—A. J. LIEBLING, *A NEUTRAL CORNER*

This is the house that Phil Nurse built. It's called the Wat, which means *temple* in Thai. Located in Chinatown, NYC, the space used to be a sweatshop until some developer realized it would be a crime against the laws of Manhattan real estate to waste exposed brick and hardwood floors on illegal Nanjing immigrants sewing Tommy Hilfiger knockoffs.

If the cast of *Extreme Makeover: Dojo Edition* had been asked to redesign a Muay Thai gym, this is what it would have looked like. Next to the elevator was a cistern filled with flower petals floating in water. The water faucets in the bathrooms were made of bamboo. Everything was placed exactly so, including the ring and the heavy bags. As I toured the studio, I could see that everything was functional but slightly precious in a way—unlike most gyms, which more closely resemble a bomb shelter—that reflected, as I'd learn, both Phil's fastidiousness and sense of style.

The hallway to the main gym was covered in photos and championship belts from Phil's fighting career. A trophy wall always adds a touch of vanity, which is a danger if the product you have to sell is yourself (see also: memoirists). But unlike many martial arts instructors, he had the record to justify it: Phil was both the British and the European welterweight champion. He would have won a world championship if it hadn't been for a controversial referee decision and a career-ending injury: His left forearm was shattered when blocking a kick. He finished the fight with one good arm, but it took two years of surgery to recover, during which he turned his focus toward teaching.

After I explained to the guy at the front desk why I had come, he excused himself, went into Phil's office, an elevated cubbyhole behind the front desk, returned, and ushered me in. Having done my research, I already knew that Phil Nurse was the son of Barbadian parents who had immigrated to England, that he was five foot seven and 160 pounds, and that he had a shaved head. What caught me were his preternaturally calm eyes, which seemed, unusually for an Afro-Caribbean, to fluctuate in color between blue, green, and gray.

After introductions, I said, "John Danaher says you're the best Muay Thai coach in the city."

Smiling at the flattery, Phil replied, "You're working with John? How is he?"

"He's good, he's good," I replied. "Tough. He's been twisting me into knots for the last few months."

"Give him my best and tell him I'm coming over to Renzo's to study jiu-jitsu with him."

"I will."

"So do you want to learn traditional Muay Thai or MMA Muay Thai?"

This was a tricky question. Many traditional martial arts instructors resent MMA's eclipsing popularity and are offended by its shallow materialism. In response, MMA proponents accuse many traditional martial arts of being filled with mystical nonsense that has been proven in the cage to be at best inferior and at worst useless.

"Whichever style you want to teach me, Coach," I said.

"Is the goal of your book to fight in a Muay Thai or an MMA match?"

"MMA."

"Oh, then I'll teach you MMA Muay Thai," he said, much to my relief.

"So what is the difference?"

"Lots, but briefly, in traditional Muay Thai, fighters stand straight and tall, almost on their toes. In MMA, you have to bend your knees and lean forward to defend against takedowns. There are more leg kicks and less head kicks for the same reason."

"Makes sense."

"Let me check my schedule and we'll set you up for some private lessons."

I went to the front desk to buy a package of ten private lessons.

"It'll be one hundred fifty dollars per class," the manager told me.

Overhearing this, Phil called the manager into his office. When the manager came back, he said, "We can do it for one hundred twenty-five dollars per class, and that will include a couple of free Wat T-shirts."

I always admire individuals who are smart enough to charm journalists. We always write nicer things about people who give us swag.

For our first private lesson, Phil started the class by directing me to the ring. "We'll just do strikes to the body, so you can get a sense of the rhythm."

I had an eight-inch reach advantage on Phil and used to think I was a pretty good kickboxer. I couldn't lay a glove on him. He was like greased lightning. He danced like a butterfly and stung like a bee.

After the round, I said, "You don't move like a traditional Muay Thai fighter." Phil held his hands and shuffled his feet like a Muhammad Ali, whereas Thai fighters lurch forward with their arms outstretched like the walking dead—zombie fu.

"I can fight like they do," Phil said. "But I spent three years as a professional boxer. So I combine Western boxing's footwork and punches with Muay Thai's knees, elbows, and kicks."

"I was just in Thailand and went to the fights. The amazing thing was they never take a step back unless they absolutely have to. It's like it would be dishonorable to retreat."

"My philosophy is hit and don't get hit."

"Mine is hit and run," I said, smiling.

After each round, Phil would explain the tactics he had used against me. His mantra was that fights are won or lost in the mind. His big distinction was between smart and dumb fighters. "Dumb fighters fight like this," he said, and then charged forward swinging wildly. "They brawl. They don't think. Smart fighters deceive their opponents. They trick them into doing what they want them to do. They are two steps ahead. When I had you against the ropes I tagged you a few times and then backed away. I didn't go in for the finish. Why?"

"A sense of mercy?"

"Someone in his first fight, maybe he panics and quits," Phil said. "But a veteran fighter is most dangerous when he is hurt. He will lash out with everything he has left. So I put you against the ropes and then backed away to be safe. I let you out, made you miss, frustrated you, made you use your last bits of energy. In your mind it felt hopeless. At that point in a real fight, I would have knocked you back against the ropes and finished you."

The bell rang for the second round. He continued to pepper me as I swung wildly and repeatedly missed. He kept this up for three more rounds until my head was spinning and I was on the verge of collapse.

"One more round," he said.

Over the months, Phil did that so often I finally accused him of being a plus-one coach, waiting until I was gassed out before demanding "one more." "Plus-one?!" Phil protested. "I'm a plus-ten coach!"

Next, Phil wanted to see my skill level with Muay Thai's basic striking techniques. Unlike most other styles of kickboxing, which allow strikes only from the hands and feet, modern Muay Thai, codified in 1921, allows attacks with the hands, feet, elbows, and knees, thus earning it the nickname "The Art of the Eight Limbs." Since the unified rules of mixed martial arts allow strikes from the hands, feet, elbows, and knees, Muay Thai became the dominant kickboxing style for the sport, overshadowing other striking styles like karate, tae kwon do, san shou, and so on.

Styles make fights, but rules make styles.

Muay Thai has the four punches of Western boxing: jab/cross (front), hook (side), uppercut (bottom), overhand or haymaker (top). It adds two more: the spinning back fist (see: Shonie Carter vs. Matt Serra, UFC 31) and the Superman punch (GSP vs. Matt Hughes, UFC 65). Of these, the Superman punch is the most interesting—and Phil's favorite—because the fighter leaps forward into the air like Superman while throwing a jab or a cross, thus allowing him to hit and not be hit.

Muay Thai has a multitude of kicks but only two are used frequently. The push kick, or teep, and the roundhouse, or shin kick. The teep has two purposes. When used with the front leg it is like a jab and is used defensively to keep an opponent away. When used with a back leg, it looks like a fireman kicking open a locked door and is used to blast an opponent backward.

The shin kick, which can be aimed at an opponent's thigh (low), torso (medium), or head (high), has only one purpose: damage. And it represents Muay Thai's biggest contribution to MMA. Unlike the flat, fragile foot, the shinbone has an edge that when hardened through proper training and landed on an opponent at the proper angle, cuts into the muscle. A few good low shin kicks and a fighter will be unable to put weight on that leg; a few more and he'll be unable to stand (see: Marco Ruas vs. Paul Varelans, UFC 7). Representing about ninety percent of the kicks in MMA, low shin kicks are the workhorses. The much rarer high head kicks are the flashy highlight reel showhorses.

For knees, there was the roundhouse, the thrust, the uppercut, and the fan favorite flying knee (see: B.J. Penn vs. Sean Sherk, UFC 84). Being attached to the arm, the elbow strikes are the same as punches, only the range is shorter and the bone harder. The key, as Phil explained to me, is that the elbow strike is less a Jim Brown forearm shiver and more a slicing attack. With their pointy tips, elbows are the straight razors of the human body and are responsible for the majority of the nasty gashes that have given MMA its blood sport reputation (see: Joe Stevenson vs. Yves Edwards, UFC 61). As a result, elbow strikes are the subject of controversy. Even the Japanese banned them, and these are the same people who allowed soccer kicks to the head of a downed opponent. But Dana White, hallowed be his name, stands strong for this slasher mov(i)e.

Having run through each technique in the canon, Phil was eager to show me some of his special combinations. Any dumb fighter can learn how to punch and kick. A smart fighter knows how to combine them to confuse and confound his opponent. A smart fighter sets bear traps and leads his opponent into his jaws.

"I like to establish the leg kick," Phil said, tapping me, by his standards, lightly on my thigh with his shin. It felt like I had been hit by a baseball bat. "I do this a couple of times and then what are you going to do?"

"Check it," I said, raising my leg to block.

"That's when I switch the shin kick to a push kick," he said, knocking me back four feet. "Next time, what are you going to do?"

"Block it away with my hand."

"Right, so you check the fake shin kick, I switch to a fake push kick, which you try to block," he said, as he demonstrated. "But now your hands are down away from your face, so I switch to a Superman punch."

Mercifully, he pulled the punch a fraction of an inch from my nose.

As I tried and failed to put a series of combos together (it's difficult to maintain the proper balance), Phil warmly retold one of his favorite war stories. It was clear he missed competing.

"I was up against this Dutch fighter and I used that combo a couple of times." Phil smiled. "He got so frustrated that he threw his arms up in the air, turned his back on me, climbed out of the ropes, and walked away in the middle of the round."

"You're kidding me," I said. "I've never heard of anything like that."

"I know. His coaches were so shocked it took them a second before they ran and dragged him back to the ring."

Phil was Loki, the fighter as trickster.

"Stand there," Phil said, as he walked behind me.

This made me nervous. You're never supposed to turn your back on your opponent in the ring (see: *Million Dollar Baby*). Phil jumped up and wrapped his arms and legs around my torso like a monkey backpack. I groaned under the weight.

"Now, I want you to go down to your hands and knees, lie flat, roll over, then stand back up."

"Roll over with you still on my back?"

"Right. Ten times."

I understood the purpose of the drill. The rear naked choke is such an effective and common submission that MMA fighters frequently need to shake off an opponent clinging to their back.

"Okay, Coach."

I did it once fairly easily, but by the second time, my legs were quivering. By the third, I was straining to get to my feet. By the fourth, I was straining to get to my knees. By the fifth, I was certain I'd lose my balance, fall backward, and injure Phil, myself, or both. Mostly I was worried about myself; I figured Phil had it coming.

"Cooooaaaach," I pleaded.

"You can do this," he said. "I make Georges do twenty in between rounds."

At eight, even Phil conceded that I was done.

"Okay, that's enough for today."

Phil carefully spread a white towel on the wooden floor and said, "Lie down on your stomach."

Assuming we were done, I was hoping for a rubdown. I should have known better.

"Now pull yourself," Phil said, "using only your arms, to the other end of the gym and back five times."

Certain he was joking, I said, "If you want the floors cleaned, wouldn't it be more efficient if you just gave me a mop?"

"You're funny," he said.

The first time back and forth wasn't so bad, but as my sweat slowly drenched the towel it became like swimming through the post-BP Gulf of Mexico.

"You okay, Matt?" Phil asked in a singsong tone.

"How many of these do you make GSP do?" I asked with hatred in my heart.

"Twenty-five. Now keep going."

■ ■ ■

A martial arts studio's quality of life is directly correlated to the number of female students. The more the merrier. And the Wat had the most of any I'd ever trained at, nearly half. As a result, it was devoid of the chest-thumping, cock-of-the-walk, testosterone-infused machismo that saturates too many fight gyms.

"I like the vibe of your school," I told Phil once. "No macho bullshit."

"Yeah, sometimes I'll get a guy like that who comes in here all *grrrr*," Phil said. "Usually they calm down. If they don't I'll have them spar with me and check one of their kicks with my shin out. That sorts them out."

Phil embodied the spirit of the gym. He was always upbeat and positive. In a year of training with him, I never saw him get angry. At worst, he'd get annoyed, usually with his nephew, who was frequently tardy. He was like a walking Zoloft commercial.

"I keep getting these angry young men who want me to train them for MMA," Phil said to me once. "And they are so full of rage."

"There are a lot of guys with bad childhood memories."

"I guess," he said, seeming genuinely puzzled.

"You have any?" I asked.

"Hmm, let me think." He paused, looking inward.

I burst out laughing. "If you have to think about it, you didn't."

"I don't know," Phil said, still considering it. "We didn't have much money growing up, but I was always good at sports. Faster than the other kids, so I was popular."

"You like your father?"

"He was strict. He'd always say, 'I'm not your friend; I'm your father.' But we got on. He came over to America and helped me renovate this gym. Construction was his vocation."

Without any daddy issues, almost unheard of in MMA, and without any primal wounds, Phil was never psychologically compelled to get into fighting. It happened by accident. "Like all kids in England I wanted to be a football, um, you know, soccer player. I was fast. But I tore up my knee. Someone told me martial arts would be a good way to rehab it. I tried Shotokan karate. But it was just marching back and forth on a mat over and over again. Same moves. Very stiff. It bored me. Then a friend took me to a Muay Thai match. It looked exciting. I start training and got addicted."

A lot of young men think fighting is exciting for a short period of time, then someone kicks their ass and they find easier ways to pass the time. Very few stick with it long enough to rise to the top. It wasn't rage that drove Phil but an extremely competitive spirit. He just really, really hates to lose.

"My top students, not often but maybe once a year, want to see if they can take the old man," he told me in one of our later practices. "They aren't being disrespectful, but they want to test me. And then I have to show them it's my gym."

Fortunately, I experienced this only once. We were practicing the Thai clinch. In Muay Thai the goal is to lock your hands around your opponent's neck, which is called a neck tie or plum, in order to pull his head down into a knee strike (see: Anderson Silva vs. Rich Franklin, UFC 64 and 77). I had eighty pounds on Phil, but he was so much stronger that he tossed me around the ring like a rag doll. At one point, however, I managed to use my weight advantage to press him against the ropes. Out of sheer luck I stuck a knee into his stomach far harder than I had intended. He inhaled heavily. So surprised that I had finally done something right, I inadvertently grinned.

My mistake.

Phil's face went slack and his blue-green-gray eyes went opaque like a shark's. He threw me off him, drove me into the ropes, tied up my neck, and blasted a hard knee into the left side of my ribs. Crowds love a good head shot, but no pain compares to a brutal body blow. My legs melted underneath me. Before my brain could register the strike, I was on my knees, gasping for breath.

"Are you okay?" Phil asked without any sympathy.

"I'm okay, Coach," I said, dragging myself up to my feet.

"I'll avoid that side for the rest of the round," Phil said.

Within seconds he had me back against the ropes, my neck tangled in his hands, and drove another heavy knee into the right side of my ribs. Again I crumpled to the mat.

"You okay?" Phil asked, not meaning it.

"Good, Coach, no worries."

After that, on the very rare occasions I landed a good blow, I never smirked again. Of all the minor injuries I endured, bruised ribs were the worst. For two weeks I couldn't train jiu-jitsu properly (John was very sympathetic, having endured his fair share of rib injuries), laugh, or sleep for more than a few minutes at a time: Every time I switched from my back to one of my sides, the pain would wake me up.

Later I joked with Phil about that predatory change in his expression.

"Roger Huerta said the same thing to me." Phil smiled, referring to the UFC fighter who was on *Sports Illustrated*'s first MMA cover. "It was our first class. He was pushing hard to test me. And when I pushed back he started laughing. 'Do that look again,' he said. Afterward he told me that was when he knew I was a real fighter."

That look comes from somewhere deep inside a fighter's soul, a feel for the jugular, and it can't be faked—the difference between a carnivore and an herbivore. I once complimented one of his former Muay Thai instructors, who had gone over to Renzo's, by saying, "He seems like a really nice guy."

"Too nice," Phil said. "Every time he would get the advantage and start hurting his opponent, he'd immediately stop and apologize. He doesn't have the, ah, aggression—what is the phrase I'm looking for?"

"Killer instinct," I suggested.

"Sometimes when I'm working with a new student, I'll test them, push them, like Huerta did with me, to see if they have it. It's not easy, because I'm the coach and they want to be respectful, but you can see it in the eyes."

"Have you done that to me?" I asked.

"Yes," he said.

"And?"

"You have it."

"If only I had the physical talent and technical skill to go with it."

CHAPTER 8
There Will Be Blood

"A computer once beat me at chess, but it was no match for me at kickboxing."

—EMO PHILIPS

"And now I'm going to hit you with this stick," Phil said, as he pulled out a five-foot wooden staff from the large chest in his gym. It contained so many of his torture devices, I'd nicknamed it Torquemada's Trunk.

Phil's female boxing coach, Annie, was working with a client nearby. Seeing the look of horror on my face, she smiled. "For your next book, maybe you want to pick something easier to research, like gardening."

"Or war reporting," I grumbled.

Lifting the staff into the air, Phil said, "I want you to block."

For three rounds, Phil swung the pole at my thighs, chest, and head as I futilely tried to check the blows with my shins and fore-arms.

Thwack.

"Oh!"

Thwack.

"Damn!"

Thwack.

"Can we take a break, Coach?"

"No."

Truthfully, I preferred the stick to Phil's shins. The previous week I had lasted less than one round trying to block his kicks before, nearly crippled, I had to beg for mercy. Phil's shins were harder than wood.

"Growing up, my trade was auto repair," Phil explained. "During lunch breaks I used to spend thirty minutes banging my shins with a hammer."

"Did your parents think you were crazy?"

When I was at the Shaolin Temple, I studied iron forearm kung fu, which involved repeatedly banging your forearms against a tree trunk for thirty minutes a day in order to make them tough enough to block a full kick without injury. When I returned to Kansas, my father saw me practicing against a tree in the backyard. After I finished, he put his arm around my shoulder and said, "I don't know what we did wrong raising you, but whatever it was, I'm sorry."

Seeing, at the end of three rounds, that I was completely exhausted, Phil said, "Okay, one more."

Phil was a big believer in fatigue training. "No matter how knackered you are, you still have reserves left," he'd often say. "You could be flat on your back, but if you heard your sister crying out for help from across the street, you'd be up on your feet running to help her."

"You look tired," Phil said. "Are you tired?"

"No, Coach," I lied. It wouldn't have mattered if I'd told the truth.

"Let's do something easier."

It was never a good sign when he said that.

Phil climbed out of the ring, fastidiously placed the staff back in Torquemada's Trunk, and went rummaging behind the boxing ring. What he pulled out of his bag of tricks this time was a weighted, multicolored hula hoop.

I must have had a you-must-be-kidding-me look on my face, because Phil said, "It improves your core strength and the flexibility of your hips, which will increase your power."

In theory, he was correct. Very little of a punch's or a kick's power is generated by the arms or legs alone. Rapidly twisting the waist is what really generates velocity for your blows. As boxers like to say, speed kills, or as Newton explained, force equals mass times acceleration. In practice, there are hundreds of ways to increase core strength that do not involve making a middle-aged man use a multicolored hula hoop. But Phil was the coach, and I was raised to never question the coach.

Having never, at least in this life, been a prepubescent girl, this was my first time with the hula hoop. One circle of the hips and it immediately clattered to the floor. This went on for several minutes, as my curses grew increasingly vivid. Phil sat on the bench watching me and to his credit restrained himself from laughing.

Frustrated and angry, I moved in front of the wall mirror to see what I was doing wrong. The problem with hula hooping as a middle-aged man with a prominent beer gut was whether to circle the hoop below my belly or on top of it. It turned out that on top was easier since there was, in effect, a ledge holding it up. As I stared at my puffy self in the mirror, twirling my hips to hold up a multicolored hula hoop above my bloated stomach, it was all I could do to keep from crying in shame.

At some point during this humiliation, a man I'd never seen in the gym before walked in. He was long and wiry with a gaunt, craggly face and a prominent nose. His affect was so withdrawn—head down, shoulders hunched, shuffling gait—that he could have been a highly medicated patient in a mental ward.

"Hey, Daniel," Annie called out.

He smiled briefly at her, grabbed a jump rope, and asked Phil in a faint Irish accent if he could use part of the ring.

"Sure," Phil said. "We only need half of it."

As the hula hoop collapsed to the ground for the umpteenth time, I gave Phil my best pleading puppy dog look. This time it didn't require any acting.

"Okay, now get down on your knees," Phil said, casually, "and put your hands behind your back."

That has to be one of the most frightening sentences in the English language for a man to hear (right after "I'm pregnant"), because it means either you are being arrested or you've already been arrested and your cellmate is named Bubba.

"Ooo . . . kay," I said, letting the hesitation in my voice linger, "Coach."

"Now I'm going to punch you in the face," he said as he pulled on a pair of boxing gloves.

I started laughing, I hope not hysterically. "Seriously?"

"You need to learn how to take a punch. More importantly, you need to learn how not to panic, how to keep moving."

Standing over me, Phil started punching at my face. The blows weren't hard or fast, but consistent enough to bounce my brain around inside my skull.

Beyond training head movement and reaction time, this drill's deeper purpose was to rewire the fight-or-flight instinct. For the average person, the initial reaction to getting hit hard in the face is to turn away. For the average fighter, the initial reaction is to get angry and try to return the favor. Both are mistakes. The proper response is to act as if you were never hit. Show no reaction. If your opponent sees either pain or rage, he will know he hurt you, and no matter how tired he is, it will turbocharge his battery.

At first I was all flight. The first blast and I'd wince; the second and I'd turn my head; the third and I'd close my eyes and go to my happy place: a Caribbean island with fruity drinks, tiny bikinis, and no punching to the face.

"Don't turn away," Phil said. "Keep looking at me. Don't hold your breath. You must keeping breathing."

After a minute or so, I had to restrain myself from jumping to my feet and taking a swing at him. This was made much easier by the certain knowledge that Phil would clobber me before I got close to reaching him.

When the first round was over, Phil coached, "Your head movements are okay until you start to panic. You must keep breathing and keep your eyes open. It's the punch you don't see that knocks you out."

The second round I started talking to myself in my head: *Watch the punch, breathe, keep breathing. He threw a right, the left should be next. Keep looking. Breathe. Breathe.*

As I started to feel the rhythm, a calm came over me. Duck. Slip. Retreat.

Out of the corner of my eye, I noticed the Irish guy jumping rope was wearing a green T-shirt with the name of some construction company on it.

Thwack!

"Concentrate."

Chin down. Eyes on his chest. Breathe.

Then I noticed he had a gold hoop earring in his left ear. No self-respecting construction worker would be caught dead sporting a gold hoop earring. Plus his hair was too long.

Smack!

"Focus!" Phil shouted.

Breathe. Keep your eyes open. Slip the right. Here comes an upper-cut. Pull back!

He seemed familiar. Where had I seen that gold earring before? Slowly it dawned. I'd seen him on *The Oprah Winfrey Show*. He had choked up while discussing Heath Ledger's death.

Holy shit! That's Daniel fucking Day-Lewis!

Thwack. Ow! Thwack. Damn! Thwack. Ouch!

Time feels more elastic in the ring than anywhere else. When you are winning and trying to hold on to your lead, time stretches. When you are losing and trying to get back into the fight, it zips by. When you are being repeatedly hit in the head, it seems to stop.

As Phil was rattling my brain, I was trying to get my mind around the idea that I was on my knees with my hands behind my back as Europe's former Muay Thai champion repeatedly hit me in the head, while the greatest actor of his generation (and my personal favorite) was jumping rope five feet away.

Daniel fucking Day-Lewis exited the ring to go over and hit the heavy bag. When we were done, I pulled Phil to the side.

"Is that really . . . ?"

Phil smiled. "Hey, Daniel. I want you to meet Matthew. He's writing a book about me, um, well, not me, but about mixed martial arts. So he's been training with me."

I panicked. What do I call him? Phil called him Daniel but they were obviously friends. Do I say "Mr. Lewis"? Or is it "Mr. Day-Lewis"? Is Day his middle name or part of his last name?

"Good to meet you, Matthew," he said.

"You as well, Daniel," I said, flummoxed.

We fist bumped.

It is an unspoken New York City ordinance that it is deeply uncool to act uncool around celebrities. After all, while they may be internationally famous, you live in Manhattan. They should want your autograph.

But it was almost all I could do to keep from squealing like some tween bumping into Justin Bieber. As nonchalantly as I was able, I said, "So, you know, if you have any insight into Phil . . ."

"Oh, I could tell you stories," Daniel said, suddenly lighting up. "If you want to know the dirt on Phil in Sheffield, just ask me."

OMG! OMG! I just had a moment with Daniel Day-Lewis. I need to text Em.

And just as quickly, the light inside him went out and he withdrew back into his shell. He went to work the bag and I tried not to stare as I mentally relived his performance in *The Boxer*. Eventually he wandered back to the locker room.

Somehow afraid he might be able to hear through several walls, I whispered to Phil, "How do you know him?"

"He came to one of the gyms I used to teach at. We hit it off, talking about life back home. He's a really cool guy. Very real."

"Everyone says he's a little odd on set. Always stays in character."

"Really? He's always been just a regular guy with me. He tried to help out my wife, Crystal, with her acting."

"You're shitting me."

"She's a working model. She was thinking about going into acting but was having trouble with it. He was working with her about getting to a place of emotional authen . . . ah . . . authen . . . rawness. But she never felt comfortable doing that."

"Daniel Day-Lewis was your wife's acting coach?"

"He just gave her a few pointers. Why?"

"You know he won another Oscar, right?"

"Did he?"

"You haven't seen *There Will Be Blood*?"

"No, I haven't had time. Is it any good?"

"Um, yes," I said, realizing why the greatest actor of his generation choose to train at Phil's gym. At the Wat, GSP was a rock star while Daniel Day-Lewis was just Daniel, another working actor.

Daniel returned to the main gym with a new pair of sweat pants in his hand.

"Phil, these don't quite fit. Do you have any in a slightly smaller size?"

"Check in the closet next to you."

Daniel looked through the closet.

"No, there doesn't seem to be any."

"We get a shipment in at the end of the month. Check back then. We'll find something for you."

"Okay, okay," Daniel said, as he headed back to the dressing room.

"See you next time, Daniel," Phil said.

"Next time, Phil."

It was all I could do to restrain myself from crying out, "Bye, Daniel! I love you!"

CHAPTER 9
Curious Georges in the Big City

"You got to have the right boy to make a champion. But if you catch a break and get a kid who's a champion outside the ring same as inside, when you got what I call a holy man, one who will sacrifice himself, then what you got is happy work and you ain't tired all the time."

—F.X. TOOLE, "HOLY MAN"

"You should come back at five," Phil said, smiling.

"Why?"

"Georges will be here."

This was the moment I had been waiting for—an up-close-and-personal look at Georges St-Pierre in action. Having John and Phil as my coaches, it seemed like all I heard about was the living legend that was GSP.

Even worse, in attempting to indoctrinate my girl Em into the awesomeness of MMA, I had shown her a DVD of one of GSP's fights. When the camera closed in on GSP's body, Em let out an involuntary, "Oh my!" For the rest of the fight, and the next few days, all Em would talk about was how hot GSP was—until I banned it from our conversation.

I was so sick with envy of GSP's hotness and general all-around awesomeness that once (in an ill-tempered moment of annoyance) I snarled at Phil, "You and John talk about him like he's the second coming of Jesus Christ."

Shocked and slightly hurt, Phil mumbled, "He's a really nice bloke."

"I shouldn't have said that," I backtracked, contritely. "You're right."

And Phil was. In a sport that has its fair share of mentally unstable, hyper-macho, narcissistic meatheads, GSP was uncommonly polite, always ready with a kind word for nearly everyone. John once said GSP was like "a nineteenth-century French nobleman who, out of a sense of noblesse oblige, tosses out free compliments to the peasants." He almost never trash-talked and seemed nearly incapable of anger.

Except for one time.

When GSP faced Matt Serra for the second time, GSP said that he could "easily beat this guy." Taking exception, Serra responded, "Frenchy, go drink some red wine and watch a hockey game." The Canadian reporters, who were eager to stoke a blood feud, asked GSP to reply. He refused, saying simply that he'd let his "fists do the talking in the Octagon." That was as mad as anyone has ever seen GSP, until he let his fists do the talking and crushed Serra like a tin can in UFC 83.

Like many of us martial arts nerds, GSP was once a sensitive, skinny, acne-faced kid who was bullied so severely that his father enrolled him in karate classes so he could learn to defend himself. Unlike the rest of us martial arts nerds, GSP turned out to be a LeBron James–like phenom with reflexes as fast as his learning curve.

The difference between a good fighter and a great one is that while a good fighter defeats his opponents, a great one embarrasses them. Great fighters make good fighters look like amateurs.

In the ranks of the MMA's greats, GSP's only competition for best pound-for-pound fighter were Anderson Silva and Fedor Emelianenko. But Fedor's reputation had been tarnished by his management's refusal to sign with the UFC, thus allowing him to duck the best heavyweight competition. (Plus, at the time of this writing, he had recently and shockingly lost three fights in a row, ending his decade-long reign as the best heavyweight in the world.) And Anderson Silva, the mercurial artiste of MMA, often seems bored with his inferior competition and toys with them like a cat with a mouse. In contrast, GSP was always getting better and better. He out-struck strikers (Thiago Alves, UFC 100), out-wrestled wrestlers (Josh Koscheck, UFC 74), and out-jiu-jitsued jiu-jitsu masters (B.J. Penn, UFC 94). And, according to his coaches, like Phil, he hasn't even reached his full potential.

A nut-hugging fanboy like me could not miss a chance to see GSP in action.

"I'll be there," I told Phil as I was leaving.

"Say hi to John for me," Phil said. "Tell him I'm coming over to Renzo's to learn jiu-jitsu from him."

"I will."

Grabbing the E train from Chinatown to Penn Station, I walked over to Renzo's, where I found John sitting on the mat with his back against the wall.

"Phil says he's coming over to train with you," I said.

"He always says that," John said, smiling wanly. "And never does."

"GSP is in town. I'm going over to Phil's at five to watch him practice."

"You might not be seeing him at his best," John said, trying to chuckle through a thick throat.

I looked at John more closely. His face was pallid and covered in congealed sweat. He looked like stir-fried shit.

"Did you guys go out last night?" I asked.

"I left early, around the time the strawberry cheesecake arrived. So many margaritas," John sighed. "Georges stayed. No, you might not be seeing him at his best."

"You sure you're up for teaching today?"

"No worries, mate," John said, leaning his head back and breathing deeply. "Have you ever wished you had started martial arts at an earlier age?" (John didn't begin practicing jiu-jitsu until he was twenty-eight.)

"Mixed martial arts didn't exist when we were kids."

"Yeah, it's too bad," he said. "Shall we get started?"

John slowly crawled on his hands and knees to the center of the mat.

"I must feel this bad because I'm not used to it," John said. "I teach eight hours a day, but I usually go to bed early. Georges trains like a maniac for eight hours a day, parties like a rock star until dawn, and then gets up the next morning and trains just as hard. Maybe the difference is he has more experience at it than I do."

"Or maybe the difference is he's young and we're old."

"Thanks a lot. I was trying to avoid that thought."

When I first started training with John, I never had any illusions that I'd be better than him. But in that tiny childlike part of my heart that still believes anything is possible, like my next book will outsell *The Da Vinci Code*, I held out hope that if I trained hard enough, long enough, one day in the distant future I might tap John out just once. Maybe by lulling him into a false sense of security, or by catching him when he was thinking about his taxes, or by an act of an omnipotent God who takes mercy on the least of His flock.

It didn't take long for John to disabuse me of that dream, so I lowered my expectations. Maybe just once I could pass his guard. But after trying every stunt I could think of for several months, including running jumps and backflips, the limbo bar of my hopes lowered further.

All I wanted to do was last an entire class without being tapped out. I tried holding on to him for dear life. I tried rolling up into the fetal position with my arms locked around my legs. I tried asking him so many questions about his favorite topics—GSP, World War II history, modern philosophy—that class would run out before he had time to submit me.

Nothing worked until this day.

John was so hungover that he could barely summon up the will to live, let alone a desire to tap me. He still could have, but why bother. The universe is random, life is meaningless, and there is nothing before the abyss but pain, suffering, and death. Moving in a fugue state, relying entirely on instinct, John flopped me around, but just couldn't see the point of finishing. As I watched the clock out of the corner of my eye, my body started tingling, my heart racing. After months of feeling utterly helpless, like a toddler wrestling with his father, I had finally found the chink in John's armor, his Achilles' heel, his kryptonite—partying with GSP.

And so it was with high spirits, rare in those early months of training, that I left Renzo's Academy and returned to the Wat. Riding up in the elevator with me was this wiry, light-skinned black guy with gold front teeth. He strolled into the gym with this gangsta walk, complete with swaying torso and rolling shoulders—pure *New Jack City*.

A crowd had already formed around GSP. The women were at borderline Beatles-level hysterical, grabbing him for pictures and autographs.

The lady standing next to me blurted out, "He looks like the statue of David."

"If Michelangelo had given him a fake tan," I sniffed.

Finally breaking away from his fans, GSP went to the locker room. When he had changed into Affliction-brand shorts, he climbed into the ring with the gangsta from the elevator, who was equally ripped if slighter in build than GSP. Phil adjusted the ring clock. Kanye West's "Gold Digger" played over the speakers. (Music is one of the key demarcations between a fight gym and a traditional martial arts dojo.)

Hoping for less hormonal company, I moved away from the groupies to stand next to Annie, Phil's female boxing coach.

"I want five rounds of clinch," Phil ordered.

"Now we get the sexy down," Annie said.

"Oh great," I said.

"It should be illegal for either of them to wear shirts," she said. "They should be forced to walk around half-naked."

"Who is the other guy?" I asked, trying to change the subject.

"Chris," she said. "He was Phil's top fighter before he joined the navy and became a SEAL."

"No wonder he struts," I said. "He is the baddest dude in this room."

GSP and Chris began the almost ritualized clinch dance. Feints forward and back. Hands reaching out and slapping away. Grabs for the neck and twists away. Finally, they clinched, each of them trying to get the inside grip on the back of the other's neck, as they alternated throwing knees at each other. Chris used his quickness to swivel his hips to dislodge GSP's slightly stronger grip and avoid his knees. At the bell, on my scorecard GSP had edged out Chris, but it was close with no conclusive clinches or knee strikes.

"You are strong as an ox," GSP told Chris, tossing out compliments like a French-Canadian nobleman with a strong sense of noblesse oblige.

As I watched them, round after round of what was pretty much a stalemate, my mind started to wander.

Most people's greatest fear when they think of fighting is pain or injury, and they project that fear onto the fighters in the cage. But most MMA fighters' greatest fear is not hurt or harm but embarrassment and humiliation. Most MMA fighters would rather have their shattered bodies hauled off on a stretcher after a victory or at least a valiant, narrow defeat than to walk out of the cage without a scratch after being tapped or knocked out in the first thirty seconds. The last thing they want is to be a clip on their opponent's permanent highlight reel. I've watched big, strong fighters tremble with shame as they looked up at the Jumbotron while it played a loop of them being flattened by prior opponents. Losses can be lived down; highlight reels are nightmares you can never wake up from.

Besides, MMA training is so brutal that they are inured to the cuts, bruises, and strains. And the vast majority of injuries do not happen in the cage but during training camps, where the hour upon hour, day after day of tedium and exhaustion can result in the loss of concentration or focus that may end in a trip to the emergency room. In contrast, the actual fight itself (six minutes for amateurs, fifteen for pros, twenty-five for champions) is a blink of an eye compared to the training. Many fighters look forward to their matches, if for no other reason than as a relief from the torment of their camps.

A bigger fear—which is rarely discussed because it goes against the warrior ethos of the sport—is of hurting one's opponent. Most of us grow up in cultures with strong social, religious, and legal taboos against physical violence. It is difficult to overcome the internal inhibitions against lashing out. That is why you will rarely see a brawl between adult males in which the participants are not drunk, incredibly angry, or both.

You have to psych yourself up to engage in a sport that will likely hurt your opponent so MMA fighters have psychological tricks to stoke the fires of fury. Many have a reservoir of rage—the inheritance of terrible childhoods—that they can endlessly tap. For others, trash-talking helps. To many fighters, perceived slights and disrespect are fuel for the fire. To promoters, bad blood and grudge matches are catnip for the media and casual fans.

But anger is a limited, unstable tool and will take a fighter only so far. The mid-ranks of MMA are filled with enraged young men. The championship ranks are not. Almost none of the best fighters of recent years—Fedor Emelianenko, Anderson Silva, GSP, B.J. Penn, Randy Couture, Chuck Liddell—fight angry.

For some, they just happen to be members of that small percentage of the general population who fucking love a good fight. The adrenaline rush of battle is a better high than any drug. It's addictive.

This temperament can't be learned. You are either born with

this disposition or not. But you can train for the other alternative: a kind of Zen-like detachment. Instead of jacking up the emotions, you drain them away so that all is left is technique, strategy, and an intense, clear-eyed focus. It is cold-blooded and predatory, like a snake or a shark. A great fighter can hit the switch and enter this zone. Randy Couture's training partners told me they could see the shift in his eyes. So if you ever happen to be facing an opponent and see this change in expression—face flatten, eyes deaden—as I once did with Phil Nurse . . . run for the hills.

GSP is the exception to all the rules. He doesn't fight angry or detached, and he certainly doesn't love to fight. "Georges is the only person I know who is truly great at something he does not love to do," John Danaher told me. "He loves to train, but he doesn't love to fight—unlike so many fighters who hate training but love fighting."

By all accounts, GSP, who was so nervous before his first MMA fight that he didn't sleep for three days, still needs witch doctors to align his energy and coaches to hold his hand. His behavior so baffled the Brazilians at Renzo's gym, who, being Brazilians, can't understand why anyone doesn't love to fight, that one of the coaches, Gordinho, told me, "GSP is weak in the head." Robert Drysdale, one of the top three grapplers in the world, provided a kinder and more accurate interpretation: "Georges is a perfectionist. He gets worked up because he wants to do everything exactly right."

GSP was given the nickname "Rush" because in the beginning of his career he blew through his opponents so quickly (all in the first round) that it looked like he was late for an appointment. And it turns out he was. The irony was that one of the greatest pound-for-pound fighters in the world was so great—training so hard, finishing so quickly—because he would have rather been anywhere else than in the cage.

These reveries came to an end when Phil put kicking shields on both arms and called GSP over to work the pads. This I had to examine closely. I had no ground game to speak of, but my striking had a fairly solid foundation. I needed to see how it compared to GSP's.

Every fighter, no matter how modest his career, no matter how over the hill, no matter how long retired, still believes deep down inside that he's got one more in him. More than the money or the glory, that's what brings him back long after he should have counted his blessings, invested prudently, and donated a portion of his winnings to early-onset Alzheimer's research.

I was no different. It was absurd, of course. My prime was buried under fifty pounds, fifteen years, and five hundred bottles of beer on the wall. But hope defies reason.

Every morning when I'd wake up sore and tired, a voice inside my head would urge me to take the day off. "You don't want to get seriously injured in practice and then not be able to fight in the cage. It'll ruin your book project."

And every morning another voice would respond, "Now that MMA has gone mainstream, the top champs are making more than a million per fight. After taxes, that's enough to buy a house, fully fund several college tuition funds, or throw a Charlie Sheen–level hookers-and-blow party."

And so it was with bated breath that I watched GSP kick the shield.

How good is GSP?

He was so fast that Phil, who is as good at holding pads as anyone I've met, could barely keep up.

How good is GSP?

He hits so hard that a couple of times Phil winced.

How good is GSP?

In the cathedral of my heart where my hopes and dreams burn like prayer candles, one flame was snuffed out.

How good is GSP?

He did all this while desperately hungover.

GSP murders dreams. He retires hope. He makes medicine sick. Kids, you can do anything you set your mind to, unless GSP is in your weight class.

When the session was over, Phil invited me into the ring and introduced me to GSP.

How hot is GSP?

It was like he glowed from the inside, an aura of light surrounding him. He looked like a medieval painting of a saint. I've never seen anything like it.

"Matt is writing a book about me," Phil said, and then paused. "Um, well, about me and John Danaher and MMA. I'll let him explain it to you."

"I wanted to learn about MMA from the inside, so I've been studying with Phil and John."

"Of course, they are the best," GSP said, throwing out more compliments.

"I was working out with John this morning, and he looked sickly," I grinned. "You know anything about that?"

GSP ducked his head and smiled sheepishly, "Yes, well, many drinks. Too many."

"I was in Montreal for your fight. It was crazy," I said.

"Yes, yes, it was," he said. "We were under the ground waiting and the whole building was shaking. When I was fighting I could not hear my corner. I could not hear anything."

"The Canadians really came out for you."

"It felt good to win there."

He was clearly such a nice, kind person that I wanted to be the same in return. But my coaches thought he walked on water, my girlfriend thought he was smokin' hot, and my chest thought my heart had shriveled up and died.

"Well, you were certainly the *hometown* hero," I said with more of an edge than I had intended.

"I hope all people enjoyed the fight," he said, stung by my words. "I want to be champion for everyone."

He looked so hurt and vulnerable that I felt terrible. I wanted to give him a hug. I could see why his coaches wanted to protect him from the evils of the world of fame and fortune and envious journalists.

"You are, you are; you're certainly mine," I backtracked. "And it's great to have a true martial artist representing its spirit in MMA."

"Thank you."

Having ruined the moment, I excused myself so the groupies could grab his attention. When I returned from the bathroom, Phil was teasing GSP at the front desk.

"This woman keeps calling me and asking for your number. She says you two are soul mates from a past life and are meant to be together. Should I give her your number?"

"You know the type of woman I like," GSP said.

Phil blanched and dropped his head.

"Yes, Georges, I do," he said out of the side of his mouth.

I chuckled at Phil's reaction, because I did as well—and my girl isn't it.

CHAPTER 10
Fedor's Smile

"Russian soil loves, loves blood."

—ANNA AKHMATOVA

I had survived an entire lesson without John tapping me out. My irrational hope re-sprang eternal. Maybe, just maybe, I could tap him out. Obviously, I would have to wait until he was in a weakened state. A GSP bender. A death in the family. That was necessary but not sufficient. I'd also have to surprise him with a move he hadn't taught me. I went searching for a different master from a different style.

I eventually decided on sambo: Russia's national combat sport, its army's unarmed fighting style, and a clear descendant of traditional Japanese judo. The term *sambo* is an acronym for a Russian phrase that means *self-defense without weapons*, and there are two basic variations: combat and sport. Combat sambo is essentially the same as MMA. Sport sambo is the same as BJJ, except that chokes are forbidden and wrestling shoes are required.

Because chokes are banned and shoes are much easier to grab than sweaty feet, sport sambo stylists focus more attention on leg locks than BJJ players, who sneeringly call them "shoeshine boys." This gave me a very un-Christian idea. Given that John's knee was crippled, I might be able to submit him with a sambo leg attack.

For a month I trained in secret with Stephen Koepfer, who headed the American Sambo Association and patiently taught me his favorite leg submissions. Finally, the day arrived when John seemed tired and distracted.

As we start to roll, John gave me, per usual, side control. I immediately switched to the north-south (69) position. Faking an attack to his arm, I instead leapfrogged into the air and landed, butt-first, on his belly. John grunted. Having successfully achieved the element of surprise, I leaned down to grab his bad knee.

To complete the submission I needed to encircle his leg with my arms and legs, lean back, and hyperextend his knee. But as I reached for his leg, I hesitated.

I'd like to say that my conscience got the better of me. It's pretty unsportsmanlike to use someone's injury against them. But the truth is I was terrified that if I actually cranked on John's knee he might flip out and snap my neck.

John used my moment of hesitation to forcefully push me off his stomach, flip me around, and choke me for my impertinence. I tapped his arm vigorously.

Sambo lost some of its luster for me after that.

One thing did get my attention. Stephen was planning to take Team American Sambo to St. Petersburg, Russia, for the 2008 World Sambo Championships. Seeing this unique martial art in its home environment seemed an ideal way to learn more about it. Some of the best MMA fighters, like Oleg Taktarov and Feder Emelianenko, were products of the Russian sambo tradition. I arranged to travel to St. Petersburg as a reporter with the American Sambo team.

■ ■ ■

There is a Petersburger joke that requires a setup to explain. First, you need to know that the Romanov family ruled Russia before the Bolsheviks assassinated them in 1917 and moved the capital back to Moscow. Second, Grigory Romanov (no relation) was St. Petersburg's party boss back in the 1980s.

So, a worker goes into a store, only to find the shelves empty. Consumed with rage, he starts cursing, "Romanov!" A police officer arrests him and asks why he's insulting Comrade Romanov. "Because," the worker answers, "the Romanovs were in charge of Russia for three hundred years, and they couldn't store up enough food to last for even seventy."

I had a great deal of time to contemplate this joke as I waited for a press pass in the World Sambo Championships' media room the day I arrived. It consisted of four apparatchiks pretending to be working—a Soviet specialty that has apparently lived on. When I explained what I needed, I was waved away. "Sit over there." So I sat alone for two hours until I couldn't take it anymore. A heated debate followed about my name not being on the official list—"Why the fuck else do you think I'd be in this city in the winter?"—until finally they officially relented and penciled my name onto a blank sheet of paper.

If my morning was difficult, Team American Sambo's was worse.

"How's it going?" I asked Reilly Bodycomb, a hipster Manhattanite member of the team, complete with the bed-head hairstyle that Ryan Seacrest took national.

"It's a bad day for the U-S of A," he said, pointing to the arena floor. A teammate was being demolished, 12–0, by an Irish guy.

(In one of those weird quirks of international sports, the Irish men were surprisingly strong, as were the Venezuelan women, who several times managed to achieve what everyone else had come to St. Petersburg to do: beat the Russians at their own game. A miracle in icy weather, as it were.)

"Did you fight already?"

"Yeah," he replied, obviously depressed. "I was up first."

"Sorry, I was stuck trying to get a press pass. How did you do?"

"12–0."

"Oh, sorry."

He had been competing in sport sambo, which differs from combat sambo in that it doesn't allow striking. Points are awarded in an arcane system I never quite figured out, based on the difficulty of various throws and pins. The ways to lose, in descending order of humiliation, are (1) having fewer points when the ten-minute time clock runs out, (2) having your opponent rack up twelve points to zero (skunked, as we called it in high school) before time runs out, or (3) voluntarily submitting because your opponent is applying significant pressure to one of your limbs and the choices are giving up (tapping out) or having ligaments torn.

"At least he didn't tap you out."

The upside of the day was that it was something of a family reunion. It was the first time Stephen Koepher had seen his Russian coach, Alex Barakov, since the latter had to leave America five years ago. "The INS kept losing my paperwork," Alex told me three times with great regret in his voice. "I finally became tired of fighting the system."

After four days of Petersburgers' taciturn, stone-faced stoicism, sprightly sixty-eight-year-old Alex was a welcome relief from the low-level depression of this Prozac nation. It was three days into my trip before I finally saw a Petersburger smile in public (two teens teasing each other on a subway platform). In contrast, Alex was so overjoyed at seeing Koepfer again that he was a riot of laughter, jokes, and playful jostling, which in his case often involved choke holds and hip throws. He was so gracious a host, never allowing me to pay for a thing, that it was borderline embarrassing. "Americans were very generous to me when I arrived in your country with nothing," he'd say when I protested. "It's the least I can do."

Alex was the first martial arts instructor I'd ever met who spent his time strumming a guitar and singing with his students in the school's kitchen before class. It gave his club a summer camp feel. He had arranged a special class for me and had invited one of his students, Gleb, a nuclear fusion scientist with a gentle demeanor.

We went through the basic throws, pins, and defenses against unarmed and armed attacks. But what I remember most is something I'd never encountered before. "You don't have to hit an opponent to defeat him," Alex said. "You can fake it and get him to do what you want. Just remember that the attack must be constant. Motion is life; stillness is death."

He pulled Gleb aside to demonstrate. Alex faked a punch to Gleb's stomach, stopping just inches from impact, causing Gleb to pull back, then Alex faked a punch to Gleb's head, causing him to tip backward. Then he gently twisted Gleb's neck, causing him to fall to the ground.

I've learned to be suspicious of these master-disciple performances. The student has been conditioned to allow his teacher to look good, especially when an outsider is watching. So when Alex offered to demonstrate on me, I steeled myself.

He faked a punch to my groin. I doubled over and raised my left knee to block. He immediately reached down and pinched my inner thigh hard enough that I twirled in a circle and extended my left arm. Switching attacks, he pressed his right hand under my left elbow to straighten, raise, and extend it, while at the same time grabbing two of my fingers with his left, and bending them back to the point of breaking. Then he walked me, on my tippy-toes, toward the door, saying in a mock official voice to the class, "Step aside, step aside, this man has had too much to drink."

I was half Alex's age and almost twice his size, and he got me to the door like he was teaching a toddler to walk.

"This," Alex whispered to me, "is how the Soviet police used to arrest political suspects."

■ ■ ■

My other reason for traveling all the way to Russia was because I desperately wanted to watch Fedor Emelianenko compete and interview him in his beloved homeland. He was Russia's greatest sambo champion and (at the time) the world's greatest MMA heavyweight. For nearly a decade he had dominated the division without a defeat against the best heavyweights in the world, creating a legend that will not soon be surpassed. For a martial arts fanboy like me, it was a unique opportunity not to be passed up.

So great had been Fedor's dominance of sambo—three championships in the previous three years—that the Soviet-style opening ceremony was dedicated to awarding him a Russia Sportsman gold medal. So great had been his dominance that the wags at Fightlinker.com compared his continued participation in this event to Barry Bonds at a T-ball tournament.

So great had been Fedor's dominance of MMA up to this point—thirty-one wins and only one loss due to a controversial (Japanese) doctor stoppage—that he was considered unbeatable. As of this writing, he has since lost three in a row and seems on the downward slope of his incredible career. But at the time, Fedor was the most dominant fighter in the world: hitting like a Mack truck, kicking like a mule, and having the balance of a Weeble—"Weebles wobble, but they don't fall down." And he did all this in a relatively short (for a heavyweight) six-foot-tall frame that, while thick, was by no means ripped, making him look more like a Brooklyn corner-store butcher than a slaughterer of giants.

Fedor was also everything sportswriters say they want in their champions. While absolutely dominant, he was also humble, modest, and polite. He never trash-talked or got into trouble with the law. He was a patriot who fought for the honor of his country. And his hobbies were watercolor painting and Dostoyevsky scholarship. America hasn't had a champion who would even know who Dostoyevsky was, let alone read him, since Gene Tunney. Fedor was a credit to his sport, his country—heck, the human race.

But, of course, that's not what sportswriters really want in our athletes. We want quote-spewing narcissists who attend nightclubs packing loaded guns and shoot themselves in the leg. Writing nice things about good people doesn't sell as well as writing mean things about assholes. From a sales perspective, Fedor was the worst of the nice guys—not only was he bland, he was as blank as the Terminator. He entered the ring, destroyed his opponents, and left as if he were simply picking the newspaper off the lawn. And in interviews, he was, if this is possible, more vacant.

There were rare moments, however, when Fedor flashed a bemused smirk as though he recognized the absurdity of his occupation. It was a sign of a hidden vein of humor, which, since I didn't expect to get much out of our scheduled interview, I decided to mine. My goal was to make Fedor laugh.

We were supposed to talk after his last fight, which everyone assumed would be for the gold. Fedor entered the half-full arena for a semifinal match against Bulgaria's best. In the opening moments of the ten-minute contest, it was tight, but halfway through the round, the Bulgarian tossed and pinned Fedor. Despite the best efforts of the hometown ref, Fedor couldn't make up the point differential. Although we didn't realize it at the time, it was in retrospect the first signal that the impregnable Fedor had become vulnerable.

The Bulgarian team went absolutely nuts. The rest of the audience was in a state of total shock and disbelief. "Did Fedor really just lose?" asked one member of the U.S. team. We would have been less surprised if a lone gunman had shot Fedor from the stands.

"Cancel the interview," I told Ivana, my frazzled, chain-smoking interpreter.

"Why?" she asked. "He lost. It's a good story."

"How am I going to make him laugh?" I asked. "It'd be like doing stand-up at a funeral."

"What?" she asked, confused. "You've come all this way."

A good point.

"Okay, okay. . . . Let me think. . . . Confirm it."

Outside the Russian team's locker room was a line of young

boys, Fedor photos in hand, waiting for autographs. It took several knocks before we were admitted. The room was filled with burly, half-dressed Russian fighters. Fedor was in the corner in nothing but his jockey shorts. I wasn't surprised, because in his MMA fights he doesn't wear much more, but Ivana, who had no idea who Fedor was, begged out of the room.

"Tell me when he is ready for interview."

Eventually, Fedor finished his shower and dressed in jeans and an Affliction T-shirt. I went to find Ivana, who was on her umpteenth smoke break of the day.

I started with easy questions expecting easy answers. After three victories in the last three years, why did he want to fight at the Sambo championships again? "I represent Russia." Why is it important to represent Russia? "Because I'm a patriot." What does patriotism mean to you? "Love of the motherland." How do you feel about your first genuine loss in your professional career? "Not too bad. I made a small mistake, and my opponent used it against me."

Regardless of Fedor's insistence on having a translator present, his grasp of English is remarkably solid. I know because at about this point his cell phone started buzzing with incoming text messages. When I'd ask a question, he'd nod, clearly understanding what I was saying, and then check his Cyrillic texts as Ivana translated my questions.

I was running out of time.

I took my first stab at making him laugh with a question about his younger brother, Aleksander, who suffers from second-son syndrome. He had recently been telling gullible foreign journalists about hunting bears in the traditional Russian manner. (When the provoked bear rises on its hind legs, you stick a staff with a

U-shaped prong into its neck to keep it upright, and then you stab it to death with a knife.) While certainly more sporting than aerial wolf hunting, the story struck me as the kind of rural legend locals like to feed city-slicker outsiders.

Have you ever hunted a bear? "No." But your brother has, yes? "I don't know about my brother," he replied, and his head dropped in shame. "But I have never hunted a bear."

It was at this moment that I realized I had tapped into a family dynamic that Fedor found embarrassing. I had little time left. The pace of the text messages was increasing, and Fedor was increasingly focused on them and not me.

I had one arrow left in my quiver: Vladimir Putin, who idolizes and identifies with Fedor in the same way Teddy Roosevelt did John L. Sullivan. Both Fedor and Putin are Russian nationalists, painters, experts in sambo and judo, and stars of martial arts instructional videos. (Putin's is called *Let's Learn Judo with Vladimir Putin*.) Fedor's nickname is the Last Emperor, while Putin *is* Russia's latest emperor.

"I saw Vladimir Putin's judo video," I said. "What do you think of his skill level?"

"When he was young, he was on the Russian team," Fedor replied. "And I admire his talent."

"How would he do against you?"

"I am an active sportsman, a practicing sportsman. I don't know whether he is practicing now."

This was the moment I was setting him up for: "So would you let him win?"

For a second, I could almost see his brain light up as he pondered the variety of potential answers to this question and their various implications.

"I don't think it would be like competing, just practicing, just enjoying."

As he finished his sentence, he looked at me with a hand-in-the-cookie-jar expression. I smiled wide and patted him on the shoulder.

"You are very careful, very careful."

Without need of translation, he dropped his head and his shoulders started to heave up and down. Unable to hold back his delight in his artful dodge, he finally let go.

"Heh, heh, heh, heh . . . heh."

CHAPTER 11
Ring of Power

"One Ring to rule them all, One Ring to find them,
One Ring to bring them all and in the darkness
bind them."

—*THE FELLOWSHIP OF THE RING*

Early in our relationship, Em and I were walking hand in hand through Manhattan when we turned a corner and found ourselves in the Diamond District. Looking around, she scoffed, "Wedding rings are a symbol of male control. I'd never wear one."

"A ring is non-negotiable," I retorted, a little too forcefully.

Her whole body tensed.

"That said," I followed, trying to ameliorate the situation, "a dog collar is, of course, optional."

She laughed, relaxed, and let go of the death grip she had on my hand.

It was like the lobster scene in *Annie Hall*. For a nerd like me, true love is finding a woman who finds your jokes funny. In that moment I was done, but I knew I had to wait.

It took more than a year.

After returning from a conference in Wales, she said to me, "A couple of colleagues were *talking* to me. And it was awkward, because I didn't know when to tell them I had a boyfriend . . ."

The silence lingered.

"I can see the social value of having a ring on one's finger."

I am pretty slow when it comes to taking a hint, but I managed to catch this one. She was asking me to ask her to marry her. As certain as I was, it still spun in my head as we went to dinner the next night. Did I want to? Was I sure? For an hour or two I had a mini dark night of the soul. When it was done, I couldn't imagine a life without Em.

My brain began to work out the issues.

As a traditionalist, I would have visited her father and asked for permission to marry his daughter. But Em's dad had already, before his time, passed into the next life. So I called his eldest brother, Dwight, who had invited me to the Figawi sailing race that had sparked this entire adventure, and arranged a meeting for the same purpose.

Keeping it a secret from Em, I brought a bottle of Glenmorangie and caught the train to Boston. Dwight's wife cooked up a delightful meal and carefully avoided mentioning the question she knew I had come to ask. When we finished eating, she said, "I should excuse myself."

Dwight and I retreated to his study with the bottle of scotch. We made small talk over several glasses before I finally said, "I better do this now, before I lose my nerve or pass out."

I tried to make a coherent case before the emotions overcame me: "I know I should be talking to Em's father. I realize that's not possible, so that's why I'm here. To continue I, um, well, really love her. And, um, you know, I was thinking, well, er, I'm sorry, it's just that I love her, and, um—"

Dwight stopped my teary-eyed floundering.

"If you are asking what I think you are asking, then the answer is yes."

I had familial approval. The next step was the ring.

I called my little sister, Shannon, because she had gotten married three years earlier and seemed to know everyone in the city. Of course, she had a friend who was the perfect person for the job. Carolyn had worked for several years in the Diamond District and had recently set up her own company to custom design wedding rings at wholesale prices. Shannon had me at *wholesale*.

The agreement was that we would all meet at Tiffany's and then visit several of the other jewelry stores on Fifth Avenue, so Carolyn could get a sense of what I was looking for and I could get a better sense of how much money she was saving me.

Shannon and I arrived early because we have the same mother.

"What's your friend like?" I asked.

"She's pretty," my sister replied, giving me a warning look.

Gentlemen, if at all possible, I highly recommend searching for a wedding ring with two attractive younger women. The very bald and very gay clerk at Tiffany's nearly had a conniption fit trying to figure out my *Big Love* status as I asked, "And how much is the one carat?"

When he answered me I nearly had a conniption fit of my own. It's not a joke that there is a fifty to one hundred percent surcharge for a Tiffany's turquoise box, whose function seems to be to say,

"Don't ever complain about me working late. I've got payments to make."

Having been scared sufficiently straight, Carolyn assigned my homework: clarity, color, cut, and carat. To that I mentally added the fifth and most important C: cash. As a dude, I was inclined toward carat as the only characteristic that mattered. To me a wedding ring was essentially a BEWARE OF DOG sign, and therefore the bigger, the better. But I had watched enough women examine a gal pal's ring with the intensity of a psychic peering into a crystal ball to know that color, cut, and clarity were crucial. When it comes to flaws, females have 10× vision.

Having set the four-C parameters, I met with Carolyn at her Upper East Side apartment to see four of the diamonds she had picked out for my examination. "Each one is unique, and when you find the right one," she said, "it will speak to you."

It took three visits and twelve diamonds before I found my beloved. Her color was coquettish and her cut flirty. "That's the one," I said.

"When will you give it to her?" Carolyn asked.

It was October. Given our schedules, I had planned on asking during a Christmas trip to New Orleans. I wanted it to be memorable.

"You'll never last that long," she scoffed. "All of my clients think they can wait, but when they get the ring, they end up asking immediately. My last one had this elaborate plan all worked out. Instead, the day after he bought the ring, he dragged his girlfriend into Central Park and proposed there."

What a weakling, I thought.

But as soon as I brought the wedding ring home, the diamond began to speak to me. "Why are you hiding me in the sock drawer?

Em might find me. You know she likes to steal your black socks. Open my box. Aren't I pretty?"

It seemed like every day I would sneak open the box and stare at my Precious. It was only through gritted teeth and white knuckles that I managed to hold out and stick to my plan to ask Em at dinner on December 24 in the Big Easy. On that day New Orleans celebrates Réveillon—a Catholic Creole fast-breaking religious meal. When the day arrived, I put the ring into a coat pocket and took Em out to see the sights. But as we walked, my Precious felt heavier and heavier and I felt sicklier and sicklier.

"Are you okay?" Em kept asking me all day.

"I'm good, good, great," I kept saying. "Are you happy? I want you to be happy."

Each time I said this, she looked at me like I'd gone insane, which only made me more nervous and nauseous.

"Maybe she'll say no," Precious whispered.

"She wouldn't have come to New Orleans if she wasn't committed."

"You never know. See how she's looking at you? What will you do, down on one bended knee, if she says she needs to think about it? How embarrassing. Maybe it's better not to ask. We could be together forever."

It says something about my mental state that I spent months picking out the restaurant and have no recollection of its name. All I remember is that my anxiety had hyperactivated my bladder. The first time I excused myself I stood in front of the bathroom mirror and said, "Pull it together, Polly. Practice your line."

"Will I, um, you, ah . . ."

Shit! I slapped myself across the face.

"Will you mally—"

Shit! I slapped myself again.

"Will you marry me?"

I wish I could have enjoyed the meal. But I lasted fewer than fifteen minutes before I was back in the bathroom re-attempting the phrase "Will you marry me?"

The third time I forgot to check under the stall door. After several times practicing my line, a guy came out and said, "It depends. How big is the ring?"

Fully humiliated, I figured I didn't have anything else to lose. I went back to our table, dropped onto one knee, and opened the box.

Even after all the practice, I still managed to screw up the line.

"Will you spend the rest of your life with me?" I asked.

"Umm." Em hesitated for a pregnant moment that nearly aborted me before saying, "Yeah."

She must have seen the crushed look on my face because she immediately followed up with: "Let me rephrase that. Yes, yes, yes, absolutely yes!"

Weeks later I asked Em if she had known I was going to ask her to marry me that day. She said, "I was desperately hoping that you were, because otherwise I needed to take you to a mental ward."

■ ■ ■

One of the trickier issues in life is when to tell the woman you have asked to marry you that you plan to abandon her.

For more than a year I had been postponing my MMA fight. If I just had a few more months, I kept telling myself, I'd be more prepared and less terrified.

I did the calendar math. On one side of the ledger, every June

Phil Nurse took a group of his students to a Muay Thai and MMA tournament in Virginia, where over the years they had done extremely well. On the other side of the ledger, the date for our wedding was set for March 14, in honor of Pi Day. (Yes, we're really that nerdy.) And we were planning a weeklong honeymoon in Iceland, in honor of the country's financial collapse and our need to find a discounted locale—tragedy tourism. The standard MMA fight camp is eight hellish weeks long. If I started mine on April 1—in honor of April Fool's Day—I'd have two months to cram for the final exam.

I could have stayed with Em and continued training in New York after the wedding. But if I was going to get ready, I desperately needed to get away from the comforts of home. John and Phil had done their heroic best to get me ready and had taught me a great deal. But training in my home city had proven extremely distracting, especially given that my home city was Manhattan, with its endless supply of diversions. I needed to get away and go someplace where I knew no one, someplace with nothing to do, someplace where I'd have no excuse but to train.

So I choose the least distracting city in America: Las Vegas.

Having made this decision, I had to decide when to tell Em.

If I told her too soon, she might end the engagement. If I sprung it on her immediately after the wedding, she might want a divorce. So I decided to tell her after the invitations were sent out when it'd be too late for her to call off the wedding but too soon for her to have a legal claim to half of my assets.

"Vegas? Vegas!" Em said, her voice rising uncharacteristically. "You are leaving me to go to Vegas?"

"I'm not leaving you," I said. "I'm taking a longish work trip."

"To Vegas."

"Vegas is the fight capital of the world. It is where the UFC is headquartered," I argued. "It's the Mecca of MMA."

"Why can't you go to Iowa instead?"

"It's already been done. Every MMA journalist goes to Bettendorf," I said. "Pat Miletich is like the Hack Whisperer."

"What am I supposed to tell my mother?"

"If I'm not ready for my MMA fight, I could end up in the hospital."

"You are leaving me for Vegas," Em said. "*I* might put you in the hospital."

The wedding was perfect and the honeymoon was lovely.* Em was none too pleased to see me go but mercifully did not send me to the emergency room.

---

* Sponsored by the Icelandic Tourist Board of North America

ACT III

MIXED MARTIAL ARTS

CHAPTER 12
You're Money, Baby

Too Dumb for New York City, Too Ugly for L.A.

—TITLE OF A WAYLON JENNINGS ALBUM

"**W**hy are you in Vegas?" asked the guy behind the rental car counter.

When I explained, he became extremely animated. "Dude, I totally love MMA. Who's your favorite fighter?"

"That's a hard question. I love Fedor, because he represents for all us chubby guys. Anderson Silva is a genius. If I could hire a ghostfighter to get in the cage and fight for me, it'd be him. He's so much better than his opponents that he'll retire with the same number of brain cells he started with. But my favorite fighter is GSP. I admire his work ethic and how he keeps improving after each fight. How about you?"

"I'm Hawaiian," he said. "So B.J. Penn is my favorite."

"He's from Hilo, right?" I asked. "I hear Hawaiians are so nuts about MMA that the best times to surf are during UFC events and the Super Bowl."

"Since you're a GSP fan, what do you think about Greasegate?" he asked, referring to the mini-scandal that erupted after GSP's last fight with B.J. Penn at UFC 94.

(Brief background: In between rounds of the GSP/Penn fight, Phil Nurse had applied Vaseline to GSP's face, which is legal in MMA because it reduces the likelihood of cuts. But then he rubbed Vaseline onto GSP's chest and shoulders, which is illegal because it makes the body greasy and difficult to grab. GSP won in dominating fashion, beating up B.J. so badly that his coaches threw in the towel after the fourth round. Penn's coaches then threw in accusations of cheating after the fight. The Nevada State Athletic Commission held formal hearings, eventually deciding not to overturn the result or sanction GSP or any of his coaches.)

"It's hard for me to be objective about Greasegate," I hedged, "because I trained for a long time with Phil."

"Do you think he actually greased GSP?" the rental car guy asked me.

"I think in the heat of the battle he made a mistake," I said. "Phil's a Muay Thai guy. In Thai kickboxing, it's legal to rub Vaseline on your fighter's body."

"You don't think he did it on purpose?"

"I know Phil. He's an honorable man, and he loves GSP. He'd never do anything on purpose to hurt his reputation."

"But it did."

"True, but GSP beat B.J. from pillar to post. Do you think the fight would have turned out any differently, grease or not?"

"Probably not."

"But hey, what do I know? B.J. is a great fighter. I hope he gets another chance against GSP to settle it." I said, trying to be conciliatory. "So, could you upgrade my car?"

"I already have."

■ ■ ■

Since the time of Bugsy Siegel, Las Vegas's success has been a tribute to the power of hydroelectric engineering and human vice. But after decades of doubling down, the city was busted. In the summer of 2009, it had the highest bankruptcy and unemployment rate in the country. The Strip was dotted with the steel-girder skeletons and empty cranes of abandoned construction sites. The style-challenged crowds of tourists were sparser and moved more slowly than in my previous visits. When I squinted from the sun's glare, it looked like the zombie apocalypse: The neon lights still flickered, but only the dead were walking.

I kept getting lost. The city had expanded so rapidly that my two-year-old Garmin GPS was hopelessly out-of-date. As I drove beyond the Strip, I noticed more payday loan outlets than banks and more adult superstores than bookstores. If drama geeks move to New York and homecoming queens to L.A., then Vegas is the destination for high school sluts.

On the radio, the most popular song was 3OH!3's "Don't Trust Me"—"Shush girl, shut your lips / Do the Helen Keller and talk with your hips." And the ads alternated between those offering legal help with foreclosures and those offering the opportunity to snap up devalued property.

Vegas is best enjoyed in short bursts, an extended weekend at most. Any longer and this scientifically designed honey trap will kidnap your soul and demand your entire bank account as ransom. If I was going to survive eight weeks, I had to live as far from the Strip as possible.

Using Craigslist, I rented a cheap room on the edge of town. The house was a Spanish colonial McMansion located in one of the many recent Vegas developments in which all the houses are nearly identical Spanish colonial McMansions.

The landlady, Carla, had gray-streaked hair and was missing her two front teeth, giving her the appearance of a benevolent witch. She owned several similar houses in the neighborhood, which I assume she had intended to flip but was forced by the crash to convert into flophouse rentals. My fellow travelers were five other dudes who were living in the various rooms on the first and second floors. Carla told me she could rent out only to guys because my next-bedroom neighbor, a 'roided-up meathead, seduced all the women. When he heard this, he chuckled, "What can I say? The strippers like me." On many nights he brought one home and proved his point.

It was going to be a long two months.

It took me several weeks to figure out Carla's other occupation. When I'd come back in the evenings, I'd often find younger women pouring out their problems to her as she seemed to be playing a game of solitaire. It struck me as a rude way to hold a conversation.

When I mentioned this to Em, she explained, "Um, Matt, she's using tarot cards."

"Maybe I should have her read my fortune," I said, "to find out if I win my fight."

"Never trust a psychic who waited too long to sell her real estate holdings."

■ ■ ■

Trying to find Xtreme Couture, I got lost again, spending an hour circling around abandoned road construction projects as my GPS (which Em nicknamed Mary and absolutely hates) squawked at me, "Recalculating." At eight in the evening I finally pulled into the parking lot of the converted warehouse.

The gym manager—a soft-spoken, laid-back, twentysomething guy with sandy hair and a square jaw—was sitting behind the front desk. He politely offered to give me a tour. Besides the amount of space and equipment, the most amazing thing to me about Xtreme Couture was that it offered training every day of the week in all four of MMA's subspecialties: boxing, Muay Thai, wrestling, and jiu-jitsu. It was one-stop shopping. In Manhattan I'd had to shuttle every day between Phil Nurse's gym and Renzo's Academy, puking my way through many a subway ride, because there was not a single MMA gym. In contrast, Vegas was a smorgasbord: Xtreme Couture, Wand Fight Gym, Striking Unlimited, Cobra Kai, TapouT. With so many places to train in such a small location, many of the top pros, like Forrest Griffin and Gina Carano, might spend their mornings working on jiu-jitsu at, say, Cobra Kai, eat lunch, and then drive a few blocks to spar in the afternoon at Xtreme Couture.

I quickly signed up for a two-month membership with the gym manager.

"Will I see you tomorrow?" he asked.

The intonation of his voice seemed vaguely familiar.

"If I can win back that five hundred at the blackjack tables tonight."

It wasn't until I had lost a hundred bucks, quit in disgust, and sworn to never gamble again that I realized who the gym manager sounded like—Randy Couture. Of course, the manager was Ryan Couture, Randy's son, and an amateur MMA fighter looking to go pro and follow in his illustrious father's footsteps. He looked exactly like a younger version of his father. As I drove home, I replayed the tour in my mind to try to remember if I had said anything particularly stupid to the son of the legendary owner of the gym.

During the months I trained there, I watched Ryan gracefully endure many of the dumb things unwittingly said to him by tourists. If Vegas is the Mecca of MMA, then Xtreme Couture is its Kaaba. Before every Vegas UFC event, thousands of rabid fans descended on the city. Visiting Xtreme Couture was part of their pilgrimage. They were often so excited they'd talk Ryan's ear off.

"Randy is just the best," one enthusiastic tourist told Ryan.

"He is very good," Ryan replied politely.

"I just love him."

"We all do in our own way."

"My brother used to wrestle with him."

"Is that so?"

"Is Randy around today?"

"No, not today."

"That's too bad," the tourist said. "I wanted him to sign something."

"Maybe if you come back tomorrow."

"How long have you been working for Randy?"

"I guess you could say my whole life."

After I got to know Ryan better and we became (occasional) sparring partners, I asked if it bothered him to live and work in his father's shadow.

"No, I'm used to it," he said. "When I wrestled in high school and would win, the kids would say, 'Do you know who his father is?' As if he was at home, teaching me everything he knew, which he wasn't."

"I have a suggestion," I said. "You should marry one of Chuck Liddell's daughters and then hyphenate your last name."

"His daughters are too young," he laughed.

"Who cares? Just think of it." I said. "It wouldn't matter who you were fighting, you'd always be the main event. They'd put your last name, Couture-Liddell, in a big bold font and your opponent's in itsy-bitsy print."

"I wouldn't even need an opponent," he said. "I could just fight myself."

"Perfect," I laughed. "It'd be like *Fight Club.*"

CHAPTER 13
Green-Light Special

"Our motto is: 'Leave your ego at the door.'"

—RANDY COUTURE, XTREME COUTURE GYM

I found Randy's motto refreshingly Zen-like. In a sport often overshadowed by the larger-than-life personality of Dana White, hallowed be his name, it was a needed reminder that martial arts at its highest level is more spiritual than materialistic.

I also found the motto slightly ironic because the first MMA fighters to walk through the door for the first pro class I watched at Randy's gym were Phil Baroni, Frank Trigg, Mark Coleman, Kevin Randleman, Junie Browning, and Jon "War Machine" Koppenhaver—the ghosts of MMA past, present, and no future. If you don't know who they are, suffice it to say that the gates of hell do not have enough coat-check room for all of their egos. But they were only the first wave of what amounted to a who's who of

MMA: Jay Hieron, Mike Pyle, Martin Kampmann, Gray Maynard, Tyson Griffin, John Alessio, Vitor Belfort, Gabriel Gonzaga, Gina Carano, Forrest Griffin, Stephan Bonnar, et cetera, et cetera.

Xtreme Couture was a fantasy camp for a fanboy like me. Over the weeks and months I'd gleefully hang around the pro practices so I could watch the most unlikely of matchups. In the ring, Forrest Griffin would be sparring against Vitor Belfort to prepare for his match against Anderson Silva. In the cage, Dan Henderson would prep with Phil Baroni for Michael Bisping. In the morning, Stephan Bonnar would come in to train for his match against Mark Coleman. In the afternoon, Mark Coleman would come in to train for his match against Stephan Bonnar. Betting on UFC fights, which everyone at the gym did, bordered on insider trading.

I was especially amazed that Vitor Belfort and Gabriel Gonzaga trained at Xtreme, because they had both been beaten by Randy, and not just beaten but broken. After Vitor Belfort's first loss to the thirty-four-year-old Randy Couture (UFC 15), the twenty-year-old Brazilian phenom was never the same again, forever tagged as an inconsistent head case: great one fight, lousy the next. After Gabriel Gonzaga's loss against the forty-four-year-old Randy Couture (UFC 77), the thirty-year-old heavyweight, who was considered the prohibitive favorite, was never the same again, losing four of his next seven matches.

Seeing two of Randy's vanquished happily enter his gym to train daily with the guy who cost them not only a piece of their souls but millions of dollars in future winnings, all I could think was: *How cool is Randy Couture?*

He's so cool that even his victims want to be around him.

How cool is Randy Couture?

When I first arrived, Randy was off in Hollywood filming Sly Stallone's *The Expendables*, the story of a group of aging B-movie action stars—Stallone, Jason Statham, Jet Li, Dolph Lundgren, Steve Austin, Bruce Willis, Arnold Schwarzenegger—who band together for one last paycheck. For Randy it was his first big Hollywood paycheck, and yet he proved he had more acting chops than many of the veterans.

How cool is Randy Couture?

The gym was surprisingly free of overt drama, despite a setup that sounded like the perfect backdrop for an MMA-centric Spanish soap opera. At the front desk was Ryan Couture, the son from Randy's first marriage, who was seeking to carry on the family legacy. In the back office was Aimee Couture, the rebellious daughter from the first marriage who was far too hip for neon Vegas. (She eventually moved to Portland.) Running the gym and all of Randy's other business ventures was Kim Couture, the dyed-blonde bombshell third wife, who had decided to become an MMA fighter. And two weeks after my arrival, news spread across the MMA blogosphere that Randy and Kim were getting a divorce. If I hadn't read about it on the Internet, I never would have known. There was no yelling or screaming. One day Kim simply disappeared from the gym as if banished (she was), the next, Randy returned from *The Expendables* set with a bimbette younger than his daughter on his arm.

How cool is Randy Couture?

Randy comported himself with such calm, kindness, and dignity as an elder statesman of the sport that nearly every MMA fighter secretly wished he had been his father. They put him up on a pedestal, so whenever they discovered he had feet of clay (like after each divorce), it broke their hearts.

How cool is Randy Couture?

He never called an MMA fight a "fight"; he called it a "match." And he treated each like a celebration party—a lesson he had imparted to his younger teammates. "I used to fight with a lot of emotion," Jay Hieron, one of Xtreme Couture's top pros, told me. "But then Randy taught me a fight should be fun. Backstage everyone is loose—joking and laughing. I used to go into the cage angry. Now I go in smiling. And ever since, my game has gone through the roof."

How cool is Randy Couture?

Among the different types of MMA fighters, there are "gym fighters," who dominate in practice but choke in the cage, and "gamers," who often look dismal in the gym but put on their peak performance at game time. Randy is a gamer. Regularly schooled in his own school by the lowest pros on the totem pole during practice, he has repeatedly won matches no one thought he could.

"*Is that really Randy Couture?* I often think to myself when I watch him in practice," Jay Hieron said. "Then he goes into the cage and dominates."

"He's not the best athlete I've ever trained," Jake Bonacci, Xtreme Couture's strength and conditioning coach, told me. "He's not even in the top ten."

"Who is the best?" I asked.

"Vitor Belfort," he said.

"Then why is he better than Vitor?"

"Because he never breaks mentally," Jake said. "I've put him through workouts that would crush any other fighter, but he always pulls through. You can't teach that."

How cool is Randy Couture?
Randy is so cool he wins fights with the power of his mind.

■ ■ ■

One of the most important lessons I've learned about joining a new gym is to enter like a church mouse: Keep quiet, keep your head down, and keep in the shadows. Play down any past experience and let your coaches be pleasantly surprised at your ability. Puffed-up braggarts place a target on their backs.

The wisdom of this approach was brought home during the second pro class I observed. I was sitting next to Johny Hendricks, who was nursing a minor injury. A natural charmer, Johny was a two-time national wrestling champion from Oklahoma State. He was training for his first UFC match against *The Ultimate Fighter* winner Amir Sadollah, who also trained at Xtreme Couture. Betting for that fight was fierce inside the gym.

As the class was getting started, Ryan Couture walked over to Shawn Tompkins, who was at the time the gym's head pro coach, with a slightly overweight guy behind him.

"He's in town for the weekend and wants to train with the pro class," Ryan said to Shawn.

"You a pro fighter?" Shawn asked the new guy.

"Yeah," the guy said with his chin out. "I'm 10-0."

"Oh, so you got ten pro fights under your belt and no losses?"

"Yeah, that's right," he puffed.

"Well, then you should be fine," Shawn said, smirking slightly.

Johny and I were shooting the breeze when I saw out of the corner of my eye that something was off. I looked over to where all the pros were sparring to figure out what was wrong with this picture. It was the new guy. With all their years of experience,

Couture's fighters have a grace and flow to their sparring sessions. The new guy's punches were too long, his stance too wide, his movements too awkward. He was stinking up the place like a rank amateur. The only way he was 10-0 is if all his fights were against the elderly or the infirm.

It was ugly enough that I averted my eyes and went back to teasing Johny about how he might have won four national championships if only he had been smart enough to get into the University of Iowa. A bell rang, ending the round. The pros switched partners. As soon as the bell rang again to start the next round, I heard this hard, hideous thwapping sound.

When I looked over, I saw that Jay Hieron had partnered up with the new guy and was walloping him. It was brutal, relentless. And Jay was using all the tricks, backing the new guy into the kicking bags so he couldn't escape. Hitting him high and low with full force. Not holding anything back. It looked less like a sparring session and more like a gang initiation.

"What's going on?" I asked Johny.

"Didn't you see? Jay went over to Shawn to ask for the green light to beat down this weekend warrior."

"It's brutal."

"The guy is lucky he got Jay and not Mike Pyle. Mike's much more vicious."

After a particularly nasty liver shot, the weekend warrior dropped to his knees. I could tell that he was on the edge of quitting, but his pride got the better of his sense. When he stood back up, Jay battered him around the head and midsection some more, until he dropped him again.

The new guy said, "Hey, take it easy."

Jay shot back, "This is the pro class."

Then Jay went in for a takedown, picked the poor guy up over his shoulder, and body slammed him. The entire class stopped and turned to where the weekend warrior was lying flat on his back.

"I can't watch," I said.

"Eh, at least he's still conscious," Johny said. "I wasn't after I got green-lit."

"What happened?"

"I came in here my first day and was too aggressive," he said. "Too much wrestler arrogance, you know?"

"I grew up in Kansas. I know."

"So Phil Baroni asked for the green light."

"And?"

"Then he knocked me out," Johny laughed. "When I woke up I thought to myself, *That wasn't so bad. Maybe I can make it in this sport.*"

Before the pro class the next day, all the pros were talking about the previous day's green-light special. They all found it hilarious. Being the new kid at school, I didn't.

"The key to getting green-lit isn't the beat down itself," one of them said, "but if the guy has the balls to show up the next day."

Almost as if on cue, the weekend warrior from the previous day walked into the gym. Having passed the initiation ritual, he was now officially a baby gangsta. The pros looked at him, nodded, and continued telling tales of green-light specials of yore. During the class, it was clear that his skills hadn't improved, but he had proven he had balls, and so the Xtreme pros were no harder on him than they were on each other.

Many weeks later I hired Jay Hieron to give me a private lesson. (This, by the way, is how to learn from a top MMA pro and avoid a green-light beat down.) When I asked him about the incident, he was unapologetic. "You get these guys, they think they're the toughest dudes in the world. And so they just walk right into our place, our home, our church. I love guys like that. They need to be humbled."

■ ■ ■

Wisely, I kept to my church mouse strategy when signing up for my first class. I picked beginner's boxing. When it was over, the coach, Ron Frazier, told me to start taking the regular boxing classes. And with just this little confidence boost, my pride stirred, causing me to choose the regular jiu-jitsu class instead of the beginner's.

My mistake.

There are two ways to do every jiu-jitsu move: the nice way and the mean way. The nice way is to slickly slide the technique into place—one moment everything seems fine, the next you are tapping and you hardly felt anything in the process. The mean way is to grind your elbows, knees, shoulders, and head into your opponent as you apply the technique. The goal is to not only secure the submission but, in the process, to make your training partner wish he had never been paired with you.

My heart started pounding when I realized the jiu-jitsu coach for the regular class, Neil Melanson, was a proponent of the mean way.

"Don't let anyone fool you," he said. "We're in the hurt business."

I felt like interjecting, "Actually, Coach, we are in the victory business. Hurting is just the one of several means to the end." But Neil was so square-jawed and strapping at six foot four and 235 pounds of tattoos that he looked like he should be sent back eight hundred years and handed a kilt and an axe.

I kept my mouth shut.

When it was time to roll, my first partner was a bruiser.

"Sorry, you got paired with me," I said. "This is my first jiu-jitsu class."

"Yeah, so," he snarled. "I've had fourteen pro fights."

I assume he was at the amateur's night class and not training with the pros in the afternoon because he had work during the day. I also assume he didn't enjoy his job very much, because he seemed to be taking out all his frustration on me. Or perhaps he was just a bully and a dick. Whatever the reason, he mauled me so badly that Neil finally came over and told him that he couldn't use his arms.

This was worse. It hurts your body to get mauled and tapped out by someone much stronger and more skilled than you are. It crushes your pride to get mauled and tapped out by a guy who is pretending to be a double-arm amputee. After the third time he secured a choke with only his legs, he began laughing at me. I wanted to cry. I wanted my mommy.

When it came time to switch, I almost walked out, especially when I saw I was going to be paired with a hard-looking Hispanic who had a grenade tattooed on his neck. He turned out to be the perfect training partner. As soon as he realized I was a beginner, he slowed down and patiently coached me through various traps. "You want to put your left leg out." "Drop your shoulder." "That's right, pin my left arm."

Xtreme Couture had more than a dozen coaches. I needed to find the right one to shepherd me through a training camp and get me ready for a fight I wasn't ready for. I was down to seven weeks before Phil Nurse was sending his students to Virginia.

"Who do you think the best coach here is?" I asked my training partner, figuring someone so good at teaching would know.

"Joey Varner saved my life," he said simply.

When a hard-looking Hispanic with a grenade tattoo on his neck says someone saved his life, you listen. I had seen Joey the previous two days teaching several different private students. He seemed intense, engaged, full of energy, and funny.

As we were filing off the mat and the Muay Thai students were filing on for their next class, I heard a voice call out: "Someone lose a wedding ring?"

I looked down. Mine was gone, and I hadn't even noticed. My heart stopped. One of the last things you want to tell your wife is that you lost your wedding ring in Vegas. My only excuse was I had dropped so much weight since it had been fitted—from 250 to 210—that it was extremely loose on my thinner finger.

As I turned around I saw the person holding up my ring was Joey Varner. This struck me as an incredible coincidence until I got to know Joey better. He seemed to have a force field around him that bent the universe, causing inexplicable moments of kismet or synchronicity or I don't know what—something more than dumb luck or chance.

"That's mine, Coach," I said.

He put his hand with the ring into his pocket. "Maybe I should just hold on to it."

"If you do," I said, "you might as well take my wife, because she'll never forgive me."

"Nah, my harem is big enough already," he said, tossing my ring to me. "You might want to keep that somewhere safer than your finger during practice."

"Will do," I said. "So, Coach Varner—"

"Joey."

"Joey, I was wondering, if your schedule wasn't full, if I could get you to give me some private lessons."

"What's your martial arts background?"

"Not much. Just a little bit of this and that."

"Where have you trained?"

"Different places, you know, nothing special."

"You around tomorrow?"

"I'm around every day."

"Then I'll see you tomorrow at 11 A.M."

We shook hands. As I let go, Joey flashed a big smile and gave me the shaka (hang loose) sign. "Cool, bro."

CHAPTER 14
Behind the Eight Ball

"Show me a jab," Joey instructed, holding up two focus mitts. "Good, now a cross, good, hook, okay, uppercut, hmm, now a low kick, great, high kick, ho-ho, do that again."

Joey dropped his left hand and rubbed his shoulder, grimacing and smiling at the same time.

"You've got crack in that kick, crack," Joey grinned. "Where have you trained?"

"Different places," I hedged, trying not to smile. "Nothing special."

"Bullshit, you've got crack in your kicks, and a strong base," he said. "Where have you trained and for how long?"

"I trained Muay Thai with Phil Nurse for a year and a half."

"You trained with GSP's kickboxing coach?"

"Yeah," I said. "And when I was much younger I spent two years studying Chinese kickboxing with the Shaolin monks in China."

"Ha! When we first talked I thought you were another weekend warrior," Joey laughed, before checking himself. "Not that there is anything wrong with that."

"Yeah, weekend warriors are held in high esteem around here."

"Nah, there's nothing wrong with it. I was just sure you were," Joey said. "So what's your deal? Why are you here?"

"I'm writing a book about MMA. I wanted to train with the top people at different MMA camps and then get into the cage."

"So *you* are going to fight MMA?"

"It wouldn't be fair to write about other fighters if I didn't have the courage to get into the cage myself."

"When?"

"Phil Nurse is taking some of his students to an MMA tournament in about eight weeks. I want to put in a full training camp before then."

"So you're gonna do a tournament for your first competition?" he asked, incredulously. "And fight multiple opponents on the same day?"

"Assuming I win my first match."

"And you won't know anything about who you'll be fighting? You won't have studied any tapes?"

"There's no way to know who will sign up."

"That's, um, certainly..." Joey paused, "*brave.*"

"Will you help me, Coach?" I asked in my best plaintive voice.

With significant trepidation that he had a delusional fool on his hands, Joey worked me through the paces to test my skills. After the wedding planning, ceremony, and honeymoon, I hadn't trained in more than a month and was desperate to hide my loss of conditioning. Fortunately, while I was still no great shakes as a fighter, I had become an expert at distracting coaches with questions about their backgrounds. More fortunately, you didn't need to be an expert to get Joey talking. You only needed to be breathing. And it wasn't just talk. Once he got going he'd often break into hilarious MMA-centric impressions and freestyle raps.

Of Joey's impressions, my favorite was his wicked version of Mauro Ranallo, the MMA announcer who was better known by the MMA blogosphere as "the Dean of Inappropriate Metaphors." When Joey and I had spent more time together, I asked him to do it for Gina Carano, who was better known by the MMA media as "the Face of Women's MMA" because of her girl-next-door charm and good looks. Ranallo had lasciviously slobbered over her on air during one of her fights, saying, "I'd like to touch her with a twenty-five-centimeter pole." Joey's impression of Mauro had Gina doubled over, hyperventilating from laughter.

Of Joey's freestyle raps, my favorite was dedicated to the trolls who inhabit MMA forums bashing real fighters whose jockstraps they aren't qualified to carry.

Keyboard Warrior

When MMA typin'
You're as fast as lightin'
But the thought of fightin'
Is so damned frightenin'.

You're just a keyboard warrior
Playin' a part
Dreamin' of fans screamin'—
A fight voyeur with no heart.

During our first class, Joey and I bonded instantly. At the time, I thought it was because we shared similar interests, like a passion for Buddhism and the martial arts. We also discovered that we both were huge fans of Robert Jordan's Wheel of Time fantasy series.

"When do you think Jordan is going to finish his next book?" I asked Joey. "I check Amazon every six months and still nothing."

"Dude, he died in 2007," Joey said.

"You're kidding me," I said, crestfallen. "I've read something like eight thousand pages and now I'll never know how it ends. I think we need to take a moment of silence."

But in retrospect, I think we connected because our personalities were compatible. While I'm passive-aggressive—I'll smile when I'm angry and wait until later to stab you in the back (a useful quality for a reporter)—Joey was aggressive-passive. At the first sign of disrespect, he'd blow up but then feel terrible about it later. That sense of guilt he inherited from his Irish Catholic mother. ("She used to tell me, 'You can lie to me and you can lie to yourself, but you can't lie to God.'") The temper he got from his Italian father. ("He was a piece-of-shit biker who used to rough up my mom and me until I was six. Then I put him into the hospital.")

They don't grade fathers, but if your son is an MMA fighter, you fucked up.

Joey grew up in Concord, California, a wrong-side-of-the-tracks town outside of Oakland, which is a double-whammy since

Oakland is on the wrong side of the Bay. A rebellious student, he found, like a lot of poor kids from broken homes, an outlet and channel for his aggression in boxing. After winning the Golden Gloves, he turned from boxing to kickboxing, and then to MMA, because, as Willie Sutton said about robbing banks, that's where the money is. He easily won several matches in a row, but a recurring injury to his left shoulder had halted his move up the ranks. So, like a lot of injured fighters, he had shifted to coaching.

As the hour came to a close, Joey had been answering my questions and expounding for forty minutes. It was longer than I had intended to distract him, but once Joey revved up, there was no stopping him.

And so it was with a relaxed heart that I laid out my MMA equipment—twelve-ounce boxing gloves, four-ounce MMA gloves, mouthpiece, and shin guards—for our second class. Then Joey stormed into the room.

"You fucker!" Joey shouted at me.

"What wrong, Coach?" I asked, nervously. Joey was the last person at Xtreme Couture I wanted angry with me.

"You motherfucker!"

"Coach, what did I do?"

"You got me talking for forty minutes last class," he said, "so you could have it easy."

"Me? Coach, I'd never do that," I said, blinking my eyes innocently. "I was just curious about your background, you know, for the book."

"You're not fucking doing that to me again," Joey snarled. "You hear me? Now, start running."

I'll give Joey credit. It took me thirty-five minutes to get him talking this time. Then I was able to catch my breath, stand, and listen to him. While Joey enjoyed working as a coach, his goal was to move permanently into the media side of the business. He was overflowing with ambitious plans. Every month, he worked as an announcer for the Colorado-based Ring of Fire promotion. He had an MMA show in development at MTV. And he had made some film shorts and had a series of full-length features plotted out in his head that he wanted to make. "It's not if, but when" was one of Joey's favorite phrases.

Joey expounded. I stood and listened. The clock counted down. Joey elaborated. The hour passed. I pretended I didn't notice. Ten minutes over the hour passed. Joey finally turned and looked at the clock.

"You son of a bitch!" he erupted.

"What's wrong, Coach?" I asked, giving him my best hand-in-the-cookie-jar look.

"You did it to me again!"

"Me? Coach, what do you mean?"

"Just for that you're going to give me an extra forty minutes."

He ran me ragged. By the end of the overtime session I was a puddle on the floor. I crawled out of Xtreme Couture and drove back to the house where I was staying. My next-bedroom neighbor was vigorously entertaining a stripper. I put my earphones in and downloaded the latest TV show from iTunes. It was summer, so my standards had dropped from *Burn Notice* to *White Collar* to *Merlin* to *Royal Pains*. I was a crack addict scraping the pipe for another high.

"Do you smoke?" Joey asked me, fifteen minutes into our third private class.

"No, why do you ask?" I wondered.

I was bent over with my hands on my knees gasping for air.

"Look at yourself," Joey said. "You've only done fifteen light minutes and you're already doubled over. This has been a really easy class so far. My other amateur fighters would blow through this without breaking a sweat. You look like you're ready to fall over and die."

"I'm sorry, Coach."

"It's nothing to be sorry for," Joey said. "But a training camp is for fighters that are already prepared. You need a training camp to get ready for a training camp. You need to get in shape to get in shape. You know what I'm sayin'? You're behind the eight ball here. I want to help you. But I won't send a fighter into the ring who isn't ready. I've been in this game for a long time. I've seen fighters go to the hospital with broken orbital bones, broken jaws. I won't be responsible for that."

"You're the expert, Coach," I said. "What do you suggest I do?"

"Tuff-N-Uff is the best amateur MMA promotion in Vegas," Joey said. "They put on shows that are nearly as good as the pros. They are holding their next one at the end of August."

"The end of August!" I gasped. "That's nearly six months from now."

"I know, I know, brother," Joey said. "But you're behind the eight ball here. You need at least six months to be ready."

"Oh, fuck me," I said.

"I know you've got a deadline and your cash flow is probably tight," Joey said. "I'll call your editor and explain the situation to him. He can't want you to get hurt."

"Forget calling my editor," I said. "Call my wife. She was ready to kill me over leaving her for two months."

"I don't deal with wives," Joey said.

"Six months? Six months! Em is gonna murder me. It'll be a *Law & Order* episode."

"She's your wife. She can't want you to get hurt either."

"When I tell her it's going to be six months, I wouldn't be so sure . . ."

"Look on the bright side," Joey said. "You've got money problems, contract problems, and woman problems. Now you know what being an MMA fighter is really like."

■ ■ ■

Joey viewed me as a fixer-upper. I needed a paint job and my roof reshingled to look respectable for the neighbors, but my foundations were strong. And so I served as a test case to his skills as a coach, which he didn't feel were properly appreciated at Xtreme Couture. If he could turn an overweight, middle-aged writer into a semi-decent fighter, it would prove he was excellent at his job.

"What's our strategy going to be?" Joey asked me, rhetorically. He had already decided on our tactics.

For elite, well-rounded MMA fighters, strategy often depends on the opponent. For inexperienced amateurs like me, it depended on background, body type, and personality. My background was kickboxing. I had no wrestling experience and was at best a low-level blue belt in jiu-jitsu. The last place I wanted to fight was on the ground.

If I could cut from my weight at the time (205 pounds) to middleweight (185 pounds)—no guarantee, given my atrocious eating habits—I would have a height and significant reach advantage on any opponent. On the flip side, my height and my long legs meant that I had a high center of gravity, leaving me highly vulnerable to being taken down.

And then there was personality. Some fighters are trench warriors: They like to get in close and brawl. With my reach advantage, I was more of a long-range artillery specialist. I never was
comfortable with jiu-jitsu because I was never comfortable being
in such close contact with an opponent. I much preferred standing
at a distance, counter-fighting, and B-52ing from twenty thousand feet.

"Probably sprawl and brawl," I said.

MMA has three basic strategies. In the first UFCs, the Gracies proved submission grappling dominant. But MMA is a Dar-
winian struggle and the Octagon a petri dish. Quickly, opponents
evolved a strategy to counter jiu-jitsu stylists, and the Gracies
found themselves facing something they'd never encountered in
Brazil: an unemployed army of muscular, well-conditioned American amateur wrestlers who specialized in taking opponents down
and pinning them. These wrestlers didn't know how to pass the
guard but discovered they didn't need to. So jacked up on steroids
(not illegal at the time) that their massive necks and arms were
nearly invulnerable to submissions, pioneers like Mark Coleman
and his protégés Kevin Randleman and Mark Kerr simply took
their opponents to the ground, stayed inside the guard, and
pounded from that position with punches, elbows, and head butts
(legal at the time). Thus the strategy of "ground and pound" was
born.

At this point, the sport was dominated by BJJ stylists and
wrestlers. Boxers and kickboxers had little chance to keep from
being taken down and abused on their backs. The best they could
hope for was that, after enduring ten minutes of being pounded by
a massive wrestler lying on their chest, their opponent might
exhaust himself and they could stand back up and finish him off

(see: Maurice Smith vs. Mark Coleman, UFC 14). It took a hybrid—Chuck Liddell, a good college wrestler turned excellent kickboxer—to bring stand-up striking to MMA.

The most common wrestling takedown is the double leg, where you drop down, lunge toward your opponent's legs, wrap both of them up, and then tip your opponent over. It's basically a low football tackle. The defense to a double leg is called a sprawl. As your opponent dives for your legs, you kick them back to keep them out of reach while using your hands to push on his neck and shoulder to drive his head into the mat, stopping his forward momentum. It looks like you've dropped down to do a push-up off your opponent's head.

With his excellent sprawl, Chuck Liddell was rarely taken down, and his preternatural ability to pop back up like the world's most deadly jack-in-the-box meant that he could keep a fight standing. Facing a UFC light heavyweight division (205 pounds) chock-full of wrestlers and BJJ stylists with poor footwork and weak chins, he cut through them like a hot knife through butter (see: Chuck Liddell vs. Kevin Randleman, UFC 31). Thus the strategy of "sprawl and brawl" was born.

"Sprawl and brawl, yes!" Joey enthused. "Because what is your strength?"

"You mean other than my sexual charisma and movie-star looks?" I asked. "Probably my reach."

"Your strength is your length. And how do you maintain your length?" Joey asked. "How do you keep your opponent at the end of your punches and your kicks?"

"I don't know, Coach."

"Footwork."

From this point forward, I spent the first twenty minutes of each class circling left, circling right, stopping, and bouncing on my toes. Then Joey stabbed his fist out and shuffled forward as I shuffled backward to keep just outside his reach. Then he would cut off the ring and push me into a corner, and I'd have to duck a punch and circle back to the center of the ring. Over and over again until my legs and lungs burned.

"You can do this!" Joey would shout. "Say it!"

"I can do this!" I would shout back, while thinking, *I'm good enough, I'm smart enough, and doggone it, people like me.*

I had a strong foundation in kickboxing and quickly became quite good at shuffling and circling. The problem was keeping my hands up to protect my chin. "Get your hands up!" is the most common command coaches scream at their fighters, because as Chuck Liddell found out with Quinton Jackson, it doesn't matter how tough you are—one tap to the button and it's lights out. Despite this, fighters are always dropping their hands. It is easier to punch from your chest or shoulders than your chin. And every fighter thinks he is quick enough to dodge that hook to the button.

Since I'm tall and used to punching down at shorter opponents, I had a terrible habit of dropping my hands. Joey used every trick he had to reeducate me, short of sending me to a gulag.

The first time I'd do it, he'd say, "Keep your hands up, please."

The second time, he'd say in a sharper tone, "Please, keep your hands up."

The third time, he'd growl, "Keep your fucking hands up."

The fourth time, he'd smack me in the head and say, "That's why you keep your hands up."

The fifth time, he'd ask, "Do you want me to fine you twenty dollars for dropping your hands, or do you want to do twenty push-ups?"

It was a trick question. Whatever I said, he'd pick the opposite unless he guessed correctly that I was assuming he'd pick the opposite, etc. Usually I was so exhausted by the time he asked this question that I'd try to get him to fine me the twenty. At the end of six months, I owed him five hundred eighty dollars.

After class I went back to my little room, put my earphones in, and watched more awful TV. As my next-door roommate enthralled yet another pole dancer, I tried to pretend I enjoyed the TV show *Sanctuary*.

It took several days before I screwed up the courage to call Em.

"My coach, Joey, says," I pleaded, as sweat dripped off my brow, "I need to stay and keep training for an extra four months."

"I'm sorry, did I hear you right? Did you just say you're staying an extra four months in Vegas?" Em asked.

"Um, yeah, I think that's, ah, what I said."

"I can't deal with this right now. I'm going to pretend you didn't just say that."

"Okay, okay, I understand," I tried to explain. "But Joey says I'm not ready, and he's the expert. He's says if I were to get into the ring in eight weeks, I might end up in the hospital. You don't want me to get hurt, do you?

"Right now, you don't want me to answer that question."

CHAPTER 15
The Thrill Is Over

"The Irish are a very fair people, they never speak well of one another."

—JAMES BOSWELL

Joey's sparring classes were every Wednesday and Friday at noon. And so every Tuesday and Thursday night, I suffered from a bad case of the terrors. Punching pads and kicking bags were good homework, but sparring was the midterm exam—a test of how well you would do on the final. Those nights I tossed and turned in bed, stressed out and imagining the worst, unable to fall asleep. I tried sleeping pills and counting sheep, but the only thing that worked was watching *CSI: Miami*. David Caruso is my Tylenol PM. Every time he put on his sunglasses and delivered yet another of his breathy one-liners—"The verdict is in, Frank, but the jury is out"—I'd start giggling, relax, and fade off into a fitful sleep.

Still I was afraid there was something wrong with me until I quietly brought up the subject with Joey. "I used to think I was the only one, too," Joey reassured me. "But then I discovered all my teammates went through the same thing."

I nervously spent the week before my first sparring session performing a risk assessment on all of the amateurs at Xtreme Couture. Who had talent? What combinations did they like to throw? What were the potential weaknesses in their defenses?

My biggest worries were Ryan Couture (who Joey had given the gym nickname R2C2) and a twenty-one-year-old Irish kid, Phil Maloney. Ryan's stand-up techniques were smooth, fast, and powerful. Phil had showed up the week prior with his mate, Shane. These two martial arts geeks had saved up their odd-job money in Ireland for the sole purpose of traveling to America to study at Xtreme Couture for the summer. Shane was your average tae kwon do student, but Phil was something special—an original and unique striker. He moved at odd angles, punched from odd directions, and kicked with odd combinations.

Dreading it for days, the hour finally clicked noon on Wednesday for my first sparring class. Joey instructed us to shadowbox for our warm-up. The point was to practice our combinations, but the truth is we spent most of the time surreptitiously eyeing each other. In the ring were Phil, Shane, Ryan Couture, and Bryan—a fairly successful pro wrestler who went by the ring name "American Dragon." This represented an overbooked house. While Joey's eleven o'clock intermediate Muay Thai class would typically get thirty guys, all but two or three would disappear before his noon sparring session.

The next round was four-for-fours, another warm-up session. Paired up, one teammate performed a four-part combination of punches and kicks that the other tried to block and switcheroo. Each round ran for three minutes, marked by the interval timer that Joey placed next to the ring. (For the next six months, my life was divided into three-minute intervals.) My training partner was Shane. We went back and forth. Given his tae kwon do background, he had solid high kicks but dropped his hands and left his chin open to attacks.

With the warm-ups complete, we shifted to straight boxing, no kicks. This was when everyone rechecked his mouthpiece. Boxing was the round to hurt and be hurt. I found myself paired up with Bryan. It wasn't even close. I simply had too much reach and experience on him, easily knocking him around the ring. Pro wrestling is violent acrobatics, and the performers spend years learning their art, but its relation to real fighting is like figure skating to hockey.

After two rounds of boxing, we switched to kickboxing. Joey made the lineups, and he gave me Ryan first. All I remember clearly is that he clocked me with a left hook and then I went apeshit crazy. After Ryan's blow, I just started swinging wildly for the fences. Almost all of my barrage missed, but I finally caught him with a hard right cross.

Time slowed and Ryan's face came into focus. I saw his eyes dilate for a moment in surprise before they narrowed. A moment before, we were sparring as teammates; now it was serious. His face didn't tighten; it went blank, and I knew I was screwed before the next combo happened. It was a jab, cross, and hook leading to a right leg kick. I'd watched him practice it repeatedly while shadowboxing so I knew it was his favorite stand-up technique. But watching is not stopping. I retreated but not fast enough. His punches kept my guard and attention up high and then his kick landed perfectly on the nerve just above my knee. The pain shot down to my foot and up to my hip at the same moment. My left leg wasn't completely useless, but it was close. I had to limp over to the corner.

"Coach . . ." I pleaded.

"Get some ice on that," Joey said. "You've got the smoker coming up."

Gimping into the main lobby, Ryan's sister, Aimee Couture, took one look at me and asked, "How you doing, Matt?"

"Tell your brother to stop hurting me," I said in a faux-plaintive voice. "He just hits me and hits me and hits me. It's so cruel. Make him be nice to me, pretty please."

This made her crack up, which was a delight. Aimee had a wonderful laugh.

Sitting back on the benches of the gym with my leg up and the ice bag strapped to my leg, Ryan wandered past me, stopped, and asked, "You all right?"

It was one of the things I liked most about MMA fighters. They didn't mind putting a little hurt on a teammate, but they never wanted to cause an injury. They wanted to win, often desperately, but not at the expense of permanent damage. They were in the hurt game, not the injury game.

"Just tell me that I hurt you, too," I said.

"Well, my knuckles are a little sore," Ryan smirked.

"You bastard."

■ ■ ■

By Friday's sparring class, my leg still hadn't healed from the massive contusion Ryan had planted on it, but I pretended that it didn't hurt. By the kickboxing rounds, I was paired this time against Irish Phil, who was tall and lanky (six foot two and 170 pounds) and had an ideal striking style to take advantage of his reach: long, straight jabs and tricky kicks. He lit me up early with jabs and crosses, before he threw a right shin kick that looked like it was aimed at my torso. I bent and put my forearms down to block. Anticipating my reaction, he twisted his waist and raised his kick at the last moment, sending it crashing into the side of my face. As they say in boxing, it's the blow you don't see that hurts the most.

As it struck, my body took a jaunt down Queer Street. It felt like I was standing still and the gym was spinning around me. My brain performed a systems check. I could still feel my legs underneath me, but my vision was blurred. I shook my head but couldn't get my eyesight to clear. Realizing I was in trouble, I raised my left hand into the air and took a knee—a gesture used to ask for an eight count.

I had been hit plenty hard before, I had even been knocked off my feet, but I'd never had to take an eight count. It was humiliating. I knew I didn't have the hardest chin in the world, but I didn't have a glass jaw either.

When I stood back up, Phil took it easy on me. He mixed in knocking me around with coaching suggestions: "You got no head movement. Before I punch, I know exactly where your face will be." Phil was trying to be helpful, but it burned me that not only was he better, but he was so much better that he felt comfortable throwing in a few pointers. I waited until he had dropped his hands to make a suggestion and then I blasted him with a right cross.

We were back on like Donkey Kong. At some point in the foray, he landed a high left hook that knocked one of my contact lenses clean out of my right eye. I'm way past legally blind without them. Only able to see out of one eye, I had simultaneously lost peripheral vision on my right side and all depth perception. I couldn't tell how close a punch was to my face; my only way of judging it was to calculate the bend in Phil's elbow.

In the kingdom of the one-eyed, the two-eyed man is king. About ten seconds later, Phil hit me with a right hook that knocked the contact out of my left eye, leaving me doing the Helen Keller. I raised both hands in surrender.

As I stepped out of the ring in the middle of the round, Joey shouted at me, "And where the fuck are you going?"

"Phil knocked out both of my contacts," I said. "I can't see. I'm going to the bathroom to put new ones in."

"Oh, it's always something with you," Joey semi-joked. "'Joey, I'm crippled. Joey, I'm blind.'"

"Sorry, Coach."

After I'd replaced the contacts and the class was over, the boys sat around the benches teasing each other, as boys like to do. There is an odd, primal bond that occurs after men battle in a ritualized setting. Relationships are forged, hierarchies are established, friendships born. It is as intimate as you can get with another man without actually being intimate.

Given that Phil and Shane were proper Irish and Joey and I were only Irish American, we took great pleasure in doing our best Lucky Charms accents for them. While Joey was brilliant at accents, I have little talent for them. So I'd spent the last several evenings trying to up my game by working on my impression of Liam Neeson as the spokesman for the cereal.

"From when the tahm I was a wee lad to the tahm I was a mahn, this sugary sweetness has been in my hahd. The years have gotten heaviah, but Lucky Charms stay light. One bite is like living the life of Riley. By Jaysus, how could that not be good for ya?"

"You Americans find that funny?" Phil asked, slightly baffled. (This was his first trip outside of Ireland.)

"It pahses the time," I said.

Sitting on the other side of the ring were two female fighters— Gina Carano and Tasha Marzolla. They were having a lunch of plain chicken and rice since they needed to cut weight for their upcoming fights. For Gina this was crucial because she was nervously training for the biggest fight of her career against Cris "Cyborg" Santos. She had missed weight and been fined several times in the past. While we boys were simultaneously trying to amuse and one-up each other, the girls were doing what girls do: complaining about their men.

"He never wants me unless some other man wants me," Tasha said. "Then he gets jealous and suddenly I'm attractive to him."

A former *Playboy* model, Tasha had become a relatively successful kickboxer and was trying to make the switch to MMA. (Almost all female MMA fighters start in the stand-up arts, unlike the men, who usually begin in wrestling or jiu-jitsu.) Given her looks and technical skill, Tasha was a headliner and poster girl for Tuff-N-Uff's amateur events.

While I was simultaneously eavesdropping and trying to keep up with Joey's endless stream of jokes, impressions, and stories, a sweet sound caught my ear and pulled my attention away. It was the sound of someone working the heavy bag. It was a rat-a-tat-tat-thump-thump-slap. It was a beautiful melody.

The heavy bag is considered a utilitarian device, but under the right hands and feet it can be turned, like a garbage can, into a noisy, funky musical instrument. If you have trained in fight gyms long enough, you don't have to watch a fighter hit the heavy bag to know if he or she is any good—all you have to do is listen to the thump-thumps.

I looked up and saw a tiny white woman, close to fifty, with a slight upper frame and a larger backside, working the bag with punches and Thai kicks like a maestro. I looked behind me and noticed that Gina Carano had disengaged from the "men suck" discussion and was staring. And then I saw that Joey and Phil were transfixed.

"Who is that?" I asked Joey.

"Never seen her before."

This wasn't so unusual at the time. It was the week before UFC 100, and the gym was filled with newcomers who were in town for the main event.

"Where do you think she's from?" Phil asked.

"Let's see. Her style is Muay Thai," I said. "Given her age, she has to be Western European, not American. Muay Thai didn't gain a foothold here until recently. Normally, I'd guess Holland, where Muay Thai has been most popular for the longest, but if you look at her build—thin in the torso, too much junk in the trunk— I'd say the United Kingdom or perhaps, and forgive me if this is an insult to your countrywomen, Ireland."

"'Too much junk in the trunk?'" Phil asked.

"A droopy poopy," I said.

"Oh!" Phil exclaimed, lighting up to a new colloquialism.

After she was done playing the heavy bag, she wandered over in our direction. The boys effused over her. "You were amazing. You lit up the bag."

"Where are you from?" I asked.

"England," she said, and then continued to explain exactly where in an accent so thick that I couldn't understand a word. It was working class but not East Ender, and that was about the extent of my ear from the infinite variety of British class-based and regional accents.

"Is that Gina Carano?" she asked.

"It is," I said. "Would you like to meet her?"

"I studied under Master Toddy," she said.

Master Toddy was a chubby Thai master of Muay Thai who had gained a large following in England before moving to Las Vegas, where he had taught Gina, now his most famous student, how to kickbox. It was like an alumnus asking to meet the current Phi Beta Kappa.

As introductions were made, Gina said, "I was watching you hit the bag. Amazing!"

The woman didn't want a conversation so much as she wanted, like any good alumnus, to hold forth about the old days. I could barely make heads or tails of what she was saying, despite having lived in England for three years. Gina must have understood much less, but much to her credit as a person and as a respectful student of Master Toddy, she never showed any annoyance and continued to listen far longer than any other young star would have. She was the biggest female MMA star in the world, more famous than all but a handful of male MMA fighters. Steven Soderbergh was about to cast her as the lead of his next movie (*Haywire*).

I credited it to good upbringing. I reported on dozens of MMA events and attended many post-fight pressers over the previous two years, and the only fighter who ever had a father in attendance was Gina. He always glowed like a dad after his grade-school daughter's first soccer victory.

"You must have the proudest father in MMA," I once said to her. "He's always beaming after your wins."

"Oh no, he's not so much proud," Gina joked, "as he is relieved."

■ ■ ■

For the next several weeks, Ryan humbled me on a consistent basis. I'd hit him and then he'd hit me harder and more frequently. Phil was so much better that he humiliated me. On the very few occasions I accidentally connected with a solid blow, he'd smile and nod approvingly, "Good, good." When you hit a man in the ring, you want him to be hurt, you want him to be angry, you don't want him to respond like your kindergarten teacher: "Excellent, Matthew. Now try to paint inside the lines."

And worst of all, this twenty-one-year-old Irish whelp was too charming, kind, and encouraging for me to hate. After each sparring class he'd say something like, "You've got the skills. Your right hand and kick have real power. You just need to train more and scrape off the rust. Then you can drop bombs on their moms."

He used that phrase so often that I finally asked: "Drop bombs on their moms? Is that some sick IRA saying?"

"No," Phil said, looking at me funny. "Ice Cube."

A good coach doesn't just manage his fighter's training; he manages his mental state. After weeks of being smacked like a baby's bottom by Ryan and Phil, I was a twitchy wreck. It was one thing to spend a year getting tapped out in jiu-jitsu, but my background was kickboxing, so my confidence was rattled. Increasingly, I began each sparring round mentally beaten before I even started. It wasn't a question of trying to win so much as trying not to lose.

Joey had tried to mock the fear out. He did a wonderfully vicious impression of me—eyes closed, head turned, spasmodically flailing punches—to try to shock me out of my flight mode of engagement. But this only served to bring me lower. Finally seeing how down I was, Joey decided to serve some red meat—a chubby little weekend warrior named Stephen. It was like going from the bottom of the gifted class to the top of special ed. I whacked him around, stopped to give him instruction, as Phil did to me, and then knocked him around some more.

My ego soared. The truth about fighting is that you only feel as good or bad as your last result. Everything prior fades away.

Filled with a renewed sense of pride, I chatted with Joey, Phil, and Shane after the class was over.

"I dropped bombs on his mom," I said.

"Good, good, you've got the skills," Phil said.

"Enough skills for a weekend warrior," I said. "But I'm not even close to being in your league."

Shane pulled me aside and said, "You know Phil's the [something] Irish [something else] of [something else again]."

Shane had a brogue so thick that at times I thought he was speaking Gaelic.

"What did you say?"

"Phil's the five-time Irish [something] of [something else]."

"What?"

"He's the five-time Irish champion of kickboxing."

"Well, shit. Why didn't you say that before?" I asked, suddenly filled with relief. "I wouldn't have felt like such a punk for so long."

"He makes us all feel like punks," Shane replied. "He can't help himself—Phil 'The Thrill' Maloney."

■ ■ ■

As devout martial arts geeks, Shane and Phil planned to end their sojourn to America with a visit to Bruce Lee's grave in Seattle. Having spent most of the euros they had saved up for this three-month trip to America, there were planning to leave in a week.

"You know Irish Phil is a five-time national kickboxing champion," I said to Joey.

"Really?" Joey said, surprised. "Maybe I'm going to have to dot him up."

"Oh, Coach, I don't know if that's a good idea. After all, your shoulder is still injured," I said, trying to hide my Cheshire cat grin. "But he is leaving next week. So . . ."

Terrible of me to be a fire starter, I know, but I had two pressing interests. I wanted to see how good Joey was against quality opposition. And while I liked Phil, after all the beatings he'd put on me, I was looking forward to enjoying some good old-fashioned schadenfreude.

It was one of the most beautiful matches I've ever seen, made even more precious because only five people in the world got to see it. Most memorable stand-up striking matches are wars where the two opponents pound each other in a back-and-forth see-saw—one up in one round, the other up in the next—so that the crowd sits on the edge of its seat, never knowing who is going to win. (The Gatti/Ward trilogy is the premier example of this type.) Joey and Phil's contest was incredible for the purity of their defense. They danced back and forth across the Octagon, blows flying from all angles, and almost all barely missing. It was like a choreographed routine for a kung fu movie.

At one point, Phil had Joey back up against the cage, firing a half-dozen left jabs at Joey's head. (Phil was nursing a hurt right elbow.) Joey dropped his hands and went into *Matrix* bullet time. Joey slipped, dodged, and pulled back just the fraction of an inch needed to make every punch miss.

By the sound of the bell, the match was surprisingly close, but Joey had scored enough left hooks and leg kicks to clearly win the round. This was obvious to Phil, because a good fighter knows better than any member of the audience or any judge who won, although most will deny it to their dying day.

"The fucker studied my style for two months. The fucker knew the holes in my game," Phil grumbled under his breath, half joking and half furious. "He knew I couldn't punch with my right. The fucker waited until I was hurt. The fucker."

Since Joey's victory was obvious, I risked saying to him, "How does it feel having one of your students hold you to an almost standstill, Coach?"

Joey laughed and broke into freestyle:

> *Polly, what are you sippin'?*
> *Because, as they say, dear friend, you are trippin'.*
>
> *No standing still here; I was too busy slippin'*
> *All the punches he was throwin', but never hittin'.*
>
> *You, him, and me knew when I was in it—*
> *That I was the master and could end it at any minute.*

Joey continued to hold court, amusing the boys with raps and impressions, particularly one involving GSP and nipple-tweaking. Well into his monologue, perhaps thirty minutes, because few people hold court like Joey, Phil interrupted him and asked: "I was thinking of joining one of the pro stand-up classes before I go. Do you think I'm ready?"

"Oh, you'll be fine. I hold my own with all of those guys," Joey said. "Thing is, it'll be the first time they've seen you in action. Hold back. You don't want to show them up or embarrass them, *especially the top pros*, on your first day."

"All right," Phil said.

"And make sure you go to either the Tuesday or Thursday striking class," Joey said. "Those days it's only stand-up. Take-downs, grappling, and ground and pound are against the rules. Most of the pros here were collegiate wrestlers, and you aren't ready to ground fight with them. But on your feet you'll have the edge. Just make sure you hold back."

As I watched Irish Phil warm up for the Thursday pro class, a wave of concern for his well-being washed over me. I went up to Coach Shawn Tompkins and did something out of character. I issued him a warning.

"You see that kid over there?" I said, pointing at Phil. "Tall and lanky white boy, looks like the guy who asks if you want fries with that? He's a very good kickboxer. This is his first and last day in the pro class. He's leaving after this to go back home to Ireland. But he's not a weekend warrior. He's spent the last three months training with Joey, Ryan, and me in the amateur classes. That makes him a teammate of mine. And he paid his dues. I don't want to see anything happen to him. I don't want him green-lit."

Shawn looked annoyed before finally saying, "I'll look after him."

All MMA fighters like to believe that they are well rounded, and they work very hard to learn tricks from every discipline. But at this stage in the evolution of the sport most are, when push comes to shove, still basically what they first trained to be: boxers, kickboxers, wrestlers, or BJJ guys. Very few of Xtreme's pros had seen a striker quite like Phil. With his first few opponents, he dotted them up but held back and did not light them up. I watched with great pleasure for several rounds—at least I wasn't the only one in the gym who couldn't keep up with him—and then turned my attention elsewhere.

Forrest Griffin was sparring with Vitor Belfort to prepare for Anderson Silva. With his huge size and range advantage, Forrest was trying to use it aggressively. But Vitor's slick speed allowed him to slip Forrest's charges, tag him as he went by, and back away. It looked like a matador with a bull. At one point, Forrest even shook his head like a frustrated beast. I placed my bet on Silva. (I won.)

The bell rang and the pros switched partners. As I turned, my heart stopped. Phil was getting into the boxing ring with Jay Hieron. I looked over at Shawn Tompkins to make sure he hadn't given the green light. His attention was elsewhere.

While Jay's background was college wrestling, he'd added some solid boxing. He had quick hands and solid footwork. But his striking was no match for Phil's. Tapping with his jab and leg kicks, circling whenever Jay got near, Phil kept Jay at the end of his range, which was far longer than Jay's.

As I was watching, Joey walked over, "I told him to avoid the top pros. What the fuck is he doing with Jay?"

"He's winning."

"This is going to end badly."

About two minutes into the round, Jay became so frustrated that Phil kept tap, tap, tapping away at him that Jay bull-rushed Phil, breaking all the rules of the class. No fake punch up high to set up the takedown. Jay just dropped his head, charged, and tackled Phil, lifting him up by the waist and slamming him into the canvas. Taking side mount, Jay then proceeded to drop elbows onto Phil's face. This must have come as something as a surprise to Phil, as he quickly covered his head with his arms. Not only were takedowns forbidden, but ground and pound was beyond the pale.

"I told him to fucking hold back and not show them up," Joey said.

"He was trying. But he's young. He couldn't help himself."

"I hope this teaches him a lesson."

"It'll teach him that even at the age of twenty-one, he can challenge and beat some of the best pros at Couture."

"Stand-up, maybe," Joey said. "He doesn't know shit about wrestling or jits."

Perhaps sensing that the entire gym had stopped to watch Jay flagrantly violate the unwritten rules and elbow a young amateur on his first day, he eventually stopped and let Phil stand back up. Phil's face had weathered the storm better than I had feared. Jay moved forward and Phil continued to circle the ring and tap, tap, tap away at Jay.

"Phil 'The Thrill' Maloney," I said. "Someday that kid's name will be in lights."

CHAPTER 16
Girl Fight

"Girlie, tough ain't enough."

—*MILLION DOLLAR BABY*

"I want you to visualize everything before you enter the ring," Joey said to me. "I want you to see the freak show so you don't freak out before it is your turn to stand and wait for your name to be called."

"Okay," I hedged.

"Tuff-N-Uff is holding the first all-women's amateur MMA fight at the Orleans this weekend," Joey said. "It will be in the same ballroom where you'll be fighting in August."

"Okay," I hedged.

"Go and get used to the lights, the cameras, and the audience," Joey said. "Walk backstage, wait at the edge, and walk into the arena. I want you mentally prepared."

The event was called Tuff Girls and billed as "Las Vegas's first all-female amateur MMA card." The promoters had cleverly scheduled it for Friday, July 10, 2009, to catch the MMA wave crashing over the city for UFC 100 on July 11. It was like the UFC's *quinceañera* celebration, a little more than fifteen years in the making. Hundreds of media outlets and thousands upon thousands of fans had arrived early to participate in all the related events. Seven thousand showed up to the weigh-ins on Friday, and weigh-ins are boring—a procession of dehydrated men standing on a scale and flexing for the crowd. But with all these fans, the energy was electrifying.

My problem was that Em was visiting that weekend. We hadn't seen each other for three weeks, and she would much rather go to one of the many Cirque du Soleil shows that had, over the last decade, metastasized along the Strip like a middle-brow cancer. I had to talk her out of *O* and into Tuff Girls.

"Women's MMA is important for us to support," I began my pitch. "If it's hard for men to make a living at MMA, it's nearly impossible for women. Even the top stars, like Gina Carano and Cyborg Santos, only make ten cents on the dollar compared to their male counterparts. And they can only get work in the second-tier promotions. Dana White refuses to hire them, claiming that there aren't enough talented female fighters to form a whole division. Is Dana's position that different than Larry Summers's?"

"I can't even believe you said that."

"What? I'm sensitive to the struggles and aspirations of my sisters?"

"I want to see *O*."

Desperate, I busted out her kryptonite: "Joey got us two tickets for . . . *free.*"

"Fine," she said, after a long pause. "But you have to take me to a really good dinner."

If the early days of men's MMA in America were a struggle, women's MMA still has not found a stable home. The Japanese briefly flirted with an all-female tournament in 1995, but it was more spectacle than sport (the winner was a 330-pound Russian) and the league quickly folded. It wasn't until 2001 that an all-women's promotion, Smackgirl, found continued success, running shows until 2008. The first major professional women's MMA fight in America was Gina Carano's Strikeforce debut against Elaina Maxwell on December 8, 2006. Broadcast on Showtime, it was the only female fight on the card and set the standard for the future of women's MMA in America. If you were a female fighter and wanted national TV exposure, you had to fight Gina Carano, because she was the sport's first and for several years only mainstream star.

If you wanted proof for Dana White that there is a deep enough talent pool to form an all-female MMA division, you wouldn't have found it at the Tuff Girls show. The Tuff-N-Uff promoters did their best to give the show a professional feel—smoke machines, flashing lights, video cameras, and puffed-up announcers—but the skill level of the participants was painfully low. While the matches were a step above a *Jersey Shore* cat fight—no hair pulling, scratching, or slapping—they were still ugly to watch.

Before the third match, a redheaded fighter had literally skipped to the ring like Judy Garland in *The Wizard of Oz*. She then tried to get into the ring by crawling on her belly beneath the lowest rope. She got stuck, and the referee had to free her. Perhaps her opponent, a young black woman, had seen this, because when she tried to enter the ring she attempted to vault the top rope instead. Her right foot got tangled and she fell face-first into the ring, nearly knocking herself out.

When I saw that Joe Rogan, the color commentator for the UFC, was sitting in the front row, my heart sank. I prayed he'd put a positive spin on this debacle, because there are a number of very talented female fighters out there and they deserve a chance to shine. It was just that none of them were fighting that night.

To keep our spirits up, Em and I debated the differences between male and female MMA.

"Obviously hair is the big issue," Em said. "They have to figure out how to keep it from flying around."

"True, I've never seen so many white girls with cornrows since MSNBC's special on women's prisons," I said. "Did I ever tell you about the last time a guy ever wore a rattail into the Octagon?"

"No."

"Royce Gracie was facing this crazy Hawaiian named Kimo Leopoldo, who had a rattail and huge tattoo of the crucifixion on his back. Kimo was so strong and fast that Royce was having trouble securing a submission. Frustrated, Royce finally grabbed his rattail to hold his head in place and then punched him in the face so violently that he eventually ripped out the rattail."

"Gross," Em said. "Pulling hair was legal?"

"This was UFC 4. Everything but biting, eye gouging, and fish hooking was legal back then."

"No wonder MMA was outlawed," Em said.

We were in between rounds and the ring girl was strutting around the ring in her skimpy outfit.

"I don't understand what purpose they serve," Em said.

"MMA has a largely male and largely homophobic fan base that spends a large amount of money to watch buff, ripped, and sweaty men roll around with each other. Ring girls are a swift,

round-by-round reminder that we're straight, or at least pretending to be."

"So why do they need ring girls for girl fights?"

"Are you suggesting ring boys?"

"Why not? They could get some Chippendales."

"Or some Thunder from Down Under."

Em pointed to the ring, where the ring girl had nearly tripped
over one of the fighters. "Every time I see one of those ring girls in
there next to one of the female warriors, it's like watching Sarah
Palin share the same stage with Hillary Clinton."

As if to emphasize the irony, after this match was over, the
Tuff-N-Uff announcer called the event's sponsor into the ring:
"Weeeelcooome, the OOOOOWNER of the Badda Bing gentle-
men's club." And into the ring waddled an aging guido costumed
like a *Sopranos* extra. I didn't catch his name—perhaps it was Big
Pussy—because the announcer rushed it to get to: "And the
BAAAAADDA Bing giiiiiirls." Six Badda Bing strippers entered
the ring.

"You have to be kidding me," Em said. "Strippers? That's it.
I'm done."

"No, you can't," I laughed. "This is such a pure Vegas moment.
Where else in the world would the first all-female fight card be
sponsored by the Badda Bing strip club? Even if you tried, you
couldn't make this shit up."

"It's disrespectful to the fighters who, while not great, clearly
worked hard to get here," Em said.

As the strippers were prancing around the ring, an obese
Tuff-N-Uff cameraman struggled to climb into the ring. While
trapped in the ring ropes, he dropped his video equipment. When
he finally freed himself and bent over to retrieve his camera, he

flashed, like an overweight plumber, his pale white ass crack to the entire crowd.

"That's it, I'm done," Em declared. "I can't take any more of this."

"No, please, you have to wait," I said, pulling out my trump card. "I have to interview Joe Rogan before I leave. This may be my only chance."

I have to confess that I have a fanboy crush on Joe Rogan. In large part, this is because he is one of the few figures in the sport who got involved more out of love than any financial need. He is a successful stand-up comedian and TV personality—a combustible and entertaining mix of testosterone and THC. He had been a cast member of *NewsRadio* and the host of *Fear Factor* (about which he does a hilarious routine: "Dude, why are you asking me if you should eat the worms?").

While a cast member of *NewsRadio*, he had volunteered to be the backstage correspondent for the UFC during the late 1990s dark era of the sport when no celebrity wanted to be associated with it. And when Dana White, hallowed be his name, brought him back to be the color commentator, his palpable passion for MMA and sense of humor enlivened every show. When Tito Ortiz won a fight and equated his victory with that of the U.S. military ("While the troops are fighting overseas for freedom, I'm here in this cage fighting for the freedom of mixed martial arts"), Rogan gleefully mocked him on air.

So I had much love for Joe Rogan. My affection for Joe was only increased by the fact that he had come to an amateur all-women's MMA event the night before UFC 100. This was the biggest weekend in MMA history, and Rogan was MMA royalty.

He could have sold out a theater for his comedy act. He could have spent his night partying in a club that would have paid him a ridiculous amount of money just for showing up. Instead he was here.

And so I was like a shy schoolgirl with my notebook pressed to my heaving breast as I tiptoed over to Joe Rogan and introduced myself.

"Sit down, sit down." He welcomed me as if we were old friends.

"So what do you think of women fighting MMA?" I asked.

"I love it when it is a really skilled, technical match. When it's sloppy, I feel a little dirty," he laughed. "I know this is the sexist douchebag in me, because I don't mind watching sloppy male fights. Some of these female fighters tonight . . . I feel like they need a hug."

"Do you think Dana should hire women for the UFC?"

"I have no problem with it, but it's not up to me. Dana considered building a league around Gina Carano, but the pool of female fighters is too shallow."

"Don't you think that's the catch-22?" I asked. "No one wants to start an all-women league because there aren't enough talented female fighters, but there aren't enough talented female fighters because no one will start a league."

"That's true. But it'll have to start somewhere other than the UFC, which already has so many male fighters under contract that it's difficult for all of them to get regular work."

"But that could result in a rival league challenging the UFC. Some of these female match-ups, like the upcoming Strikeforce main event between Gina and Cyborg, have garnered a lot of positive media attention."

"I'm happy Gina signed with Strikeforce. I've always supported more leagues. As a fan, it's good for me."

The next match was starting, and I didn't want to keep a fan from watching. As I skipped back to Em, she asked, "How was Joe?"

"I love that guy," I said. "He redeems the sport."

CHAPTER 17
My Cup Runneth Over, Cont'd

"Nobody wants to fight a southpaw."

—ROCKY BALBOA

The clock had counted down to my smoker kickboxing match. I was nearly out of face-saving excuses. My intestines were in a riot.

"Joey says it's time for me to wrap up your gloves," eight-year-old Carlos, one of my cornerboys, informed me, holding a roll of athletic tape in his little hands.

"Okay, Carlos," I said.

"You ready?" Joey asked impatiently when my hands were finally wrapped.

I had a problem. I felt yet another urgent need to use the bathroom again, but Carlos had already taped up my gloves. Should I humiliate myself and ask Joey to unwrap my gloves or should I hold it? Was the shame or the discomfort worse?

"Coach, I kinda need to go. Is there time?"

"Is this a real pee?" Joey asked, imitating a kindergarten teacher speaking to a toddler, "Or a nervous pee?"

Trying to save face by making a joke out of it, I said in a little-boy voice, "It's a little nervous pee."

"Let's go."

As I walked toward the ring, more than a little worried I might piss my pants, I wondered, not for the first or last time, how I had gotten myself into this mess.

■ ■ ■

There were about fifty people in the crowd, mostly Xtreme Couture teammates and their friends. Students and their girlfriends milled around the ring. Several kids gathered around the kicking bags off to the side, laughing as they took turns throwing clumsy strikes. I walked past, slapping a few hands. I noticed there was an EMT crew, complete with a stretcher, ready for the worst. I did not find this comforting. A volunteer doctor who trained at Xtreme Couture stopped me and checked my eyes.

"You ready?"

"All good, Doc." When I climbed into the ring, I circled and fired off a few combinations. It was the traditional entrance, but I still felt like something between a dork and a fake as I did it.

My teammate and opponent, John, entered after me, circling and shadowboxing as I watched and Joey whispered instructions into my ear. "First round, jabs. Second round, jabs and crosses. Third round, light him up." I had a significant height and reach advantage on him, but he was much stockier, more muscular, and heavier than me. I would have to counter-fight and keep outside his range.

Our hall-of-fame referee, Randy Couture, called John and me to the center of the ring.

"Touch gloves tonight," Randy instructed us. "Three two-minute rounds, all right? Good."

There are two stances in boxing and kickboxing: orthodox (left hand and foot forward) and southpaw (right hand and foot forward). Fighters are generally taught to lead with their weaker side and keep their dominant one back for power punches and kicks. Since ninety percent of humanity is right-handed, most boxers and kickboxers are orthodox. John was the first southpaw I had ever faced.

If football is a game of inches, striking is a game of millimeters. It takes years to get the angles and timing down to slip a blow hurtling at your face. Change the stance, and all that gets thrown out the window. As the traditional boxing saying has it: "All southpaws should be drowned at birth."

Almost off the bat, southpaw John hit me with a lunging right jab. I'd never seen a right jab before. It confused me more than the impact of the punch itself. Then he hit me with a left cross, another first. It seemed to come out of nowhere. It felt like I was fighting an alien.

"Hands up, Matt!" Joey shouted. "Keep your hands up, please."

With my superior reach, I was trying to maintain range. Stick the jab and move. Stick the jab again and move. Low kicks to his legs to break up the rhythm. Combinations. It is difficult for the brain to track strikes from two different planes. So I'd fake high, hit low. Fake low, and strike high.

"He's got a lot of reach on you, son," John's corner shouted at him.

With his superior size and strength, John stalked me around the ring as I circled left and right. He needed to get inside my range; I needed to keep him at the end of it. He was the more effectively aggressive fighter. I was scoring more points.

While an Octagon is almost a circle, a boxing ring has four corners at ninety-degree angles, which makes it much easier to "cut off the ring" and trap a fighter in a corner. It doesn't seem like much of a difference watching from the outside, but inside the ring it can feel like you've been locked inside a cellar.

As I circled, I kept finding myself retreating into one of the corners. The first time John trapped me in one, I tried a thrust kick to his chest to drive him back. But he was so stocky and leaning forward so aggressively that I ended up pushing myself back into the ropes.

"Hands up! Circle! Circle!" Joey yelled. "On your toes! And breathe!"

After eating another right jab, I pushed him off me and circled away.

As the round continued, it was like Joey was in my head. As soon as he said something, I did it. "Cross," he'd say and then I'd immediately throw it. "Hands high, baby," and I'd put my hands back up. "Breathe," and I'd suck in oxygen. "Circle, circle, circle," and I'd lumber around the ring.

In the last thirty seconds, John caught me with a left hook that pinballed my brain. I took a deep breath and came back at him. Annoyed with my mistake, I threw a high right kick that landed across his cheek and followed up with a left jab.

After the bell, Randy checked my altered state briefly. Joey was all reassurance.

"Good round, good round," he said. "That's the way to do it. Keep your hands up. Keep circling. Stick to the game plan. You've got this. You're doing awesome, baby! Just breathe, breathe."

Soon after the second round began, I could tell that John was less aggressive. In between our exchanges, he stopped to inhale and exhale deeply. He was no longer stalking me and we spent more time in the center of the ring.

I felt my confidence rise enough to get a little fancier. I threw the Superman jab Phil Nurse had taught me and followed it with a leg kick.

John missed with a leg kick and ended up spinning in a circle, leaving his back wide open to me. As he was spinning, I was already throwing a right cross. It caught him behind his ear—borderline illegal if it had been intentional. But he had violated the basic rule of stand-up combat: You never turn your back on an opponent.

Angry at my blow, John stalked me again, throwing wild jabs and crosses. I circled and played defense to weather his storm, waiting for him to exhaust himself. Before it happened, he had backed me into a corner. I lifted my leg for a kick, but seeing it wasn't open I pulled it back at the last second. My mistake was that I had dropped my hands for the kick. John charged, throwing a combination of punches. The last one of them, a solid left hook, caught me flush on the button. I didn't see it coming, and it spun my skull around the space-time continuum. Time slowed and space narrowed. The room went dark, and I felt as if I were walking down a long, poorly lit tunnel.

"Get out!" a spooky voice screamed inside my head. "Get out!" It was like *The Amityville Horror*.

Then another voice in my head shouted, "Hands up, Matt! Hands up, please! Please, get your hands up! Circle on your bike! Circle!"

Through the fog, close to the rocky shore with only the lighthouse to guide me to safety, I realized it was Joey's voice. I put my hands up and circled.

As the ten-second clacker sounded, Joey shouted, "Flurry, Matt!"

No matter how long the round (two minutes for amateurs; five minutes for pros), the last ten seconds are the most important. Dating might be about first impressions, but fights are about the last. MMA judges are not renowned for their sophisticated understanding of the sport (see: Cecil Peoples). Regardless of what happened earlier in the round, you want to look busy and aggressive at the end to tilt their judgment. It was irrelevant for our smoker, since there were no judges, but this was a dry run for my MMA fight.

In that spirit, I landed a perfect right shin kick to John's head and followed it up immediately with a jab-cross combination. It had been a fight up until those last moments, but with the high kick, I stole the round.

"Yo! Yo!" Joey shouted. "Great job, Matt!"

As the ring bell sounded, I pushed myself forward to my corner. My head was fuzzy. While my brain understood on some neocortical level what Joey was saying to me, all I could translate were his facial features. He was smiling. That was good. He was pointing. That meant action. His mouth was moving. That meant something, but I had no idea what.

As I was focused on Joey, the referee tapped me on the shoulder and leaned around to look at my face. As he stared at my face, I could palpably feel the blood streaming from my nose into my mouth.

(As an aside, I discovered later that John had broken my nose. When I went to one of Xtreme Couture's favored doctors, who as a favor treated MMA fighters without health insurance off the books, he said, "There's no point in readjusting it, because as a fighter you'll just get your septum cracked again. It should heal on its own." Not exactly what you want to hear from a doctor, but he was right. My nose did reset, but for the three weeks before it did, I was literally a mouth-breather. Every morning, I'd wake up with a pillow and face covered in slobber.)

In my mind, the referee continued to stare at my face. I was terrified he would stop the fight. I was enraged he would even consider it. "Don't you dare stop this fucking match," I snarled at the ref. Then something switched in my brain. I was cursing Randy Couture! "Sorry, Randy," I said. "Sorry."

At least that is what happened inside my head. After I rewatched the video of the match much later, it is clear that Randy took a half-second look at me, patted me on the shoulder, and walked away. What I thought I had said to him my fuddled brain had completely imagined.

God bless the one-minute break between rounds. By the start of the third round I was clearheaded and ready to go again.

"Circle! Circle!" Joey shouted. "Switch directions!"

I switched directions and John missed badly on a leg kick.

"Front kick," Joey instructed.

I threw one as John attempted a right roundhouse and beat him to the crux, knocking him back several steps.

"There you go!" Joey shouted. "There you go!"

We kept exchanging, but John was growing tired. For each blow he landed, I planted two.

I drove a right shin kick into his gut. He caught it and pushed me to the ground. There are no points for throws in kickboxing, so I won the exchange. But it is never good or enjoyable to have to pick yourself off the mat. Randy grabbed my gloves to wipe them off on his shirt to remove any potential grit that might cause a cut.

As he did, I thought, for the umpteenth time that match: *Hey, that's Randy Couture!*

"Jab, head," Joey said.

Slightly reversing the order, I threw a head kick that landed flush across his skull and, to add insult to injury, added a jab to his nose. John's knees buckled and he bent over to cover himself.

The Xtreme Couture crowd of fans erupted.

It is possible I could have finished him at this point, but I was conscious of Phil Nurse's teaching that a fighter is never more dangerous than after you have hurt him. And sure enough, John came at me, swinging with desperation. He battered my defenses with jabs, hooks, and leg kicks. I covered up and circled to wait out his fury.

"Finish with a flurry!" Joey shouted.

The ten-second clacker sounded.

"Hop on him, Matt," Joey shouted. "Ten seconds! Hop on him!"

I threw a barrage of straight punches. Most glanced off John's gloves, but they kept him busy. In his distraction, I grabbed his head, pulled it down, and added a few knees.

The final bell rang.

"Hands in the air!" Joey screamed. "Take a victory lap!"

Except in the tightest of contests, most fighters who are experienced professionals know in their heart of hearts who is the victor and who is the vanquished. Still, you never know with MMA judges. It never hurts to pretend you won. I put my arms up and danced around the ring. The crowd clapped and shouted for me. I went past John, who was bent over the ring ropes, and shook his hand.

It was an in-house smoker, so there were no judges. Randy pulled us both into the center of the ring and raised both our hands. Officially, we were both winners. But that's never true in a sport as absolutely zero-sum as fighting.

"I am so fucking proud of you," Joey said. "You did everything we talked about. I am so proud of you."

"You think I won?" I asked, my fragile ego still needing some reassurance.

"Did you win? You won," he said. "You nearly knocked him out with that high kick. Just one more and it would have been over."

I was in jubilant spirits. If Joey said that I had won, then I won. He was a charmer but not a particularly good liar.

I went over to the EMT guys, shook their hands, and thanked them for their service. I high-fived teammates in the crowd.

"Nice high kicks," they all said.

I stuck around to watch Ryan Couture fight Mike, my piss buddy. Ryan beat him all across the ring and so it was a good thing he didn't have any liquid left in him.

When it was over, I went over to Randy Couture and said, "I've been sparring with your son for several weeks and he cripples my thighs with his leg kicks."

With a big smile from a proud papa, he said, "I guess it's a good thing you had a different opponent tonight."

And then Randy Couture, the most famous man in mixed martial arts, and I fist bumped. For a fan of MMA, it was the equivalent of high-fiving Abraham Lincoln. Stick a fork in me; I was done.

As I was marinating in the afterglow, Joey pulled me around to meet the Tuff-N-Uff promoters—the brothers Barry and Jeff Meyer. They were at the Xtreme smoker to scout talent. At least a third of the fighters, referees, and ringside commentators for

Tuff-N-Uff events came from Xtreme Couture. Barry and Jeff had been commodities traders before they attended UFC 1 in 1992. ("It was love at first fight," they told me.) I later teased them that in giving up commodities trading for fight promoting, they had abandoned the second riskiest profession in the country for the most.

But that night I wanted to impress. With their access to Vegas's talent pool, the Meyers staged the best amateur shows in the country, complete with ring announcers, cameramen, dry ice, and, of course, ring girls. More importantly, Barry and Jeff would be deciding whom I was matched against. In combat sports, the matchmaker is God: He determines if your career lives or dies.

"Was that okay?" I asked them. "I hope I'm worthy to be part of your show."

"If your ground game is as good as your stand-up," Jeff Meyer said to me, "you'll do great. Is it?"

"Um, yeah," I lied. "Of course."

Still, feeling pretty chuffed about myself, I trotted up to the second floor to take off my gear and clean up for Joey's birthday dinner.

As I was changing, eight-year-old Carlos came over to help me.

"You did good," he said, as he pulled off my boxing gloves.

"Thank you, Carlos."

"Those high kicks won the fight."

"I'm glad you think so."

"But you need to listen to me," Carlos said, absolutely serious. "You must keep your hands up. You took way too many punches to the face."

"You're right, Carlos," I said, deflated by the future of MMA. "I did."

■ ■ ■

My smoker happened on Joey's birthday. The Xtreme gang gathered at a nearby Chili's for his party. As we sat down I held out the bag with my gift to Joey. The afternoon before the smoker, I had tried to keep my mind busy by making him a present. In between trips to the bathroom, I had constructed a tinfoil hat complete with antennas.

I wouldn't say that Joey was a committed conspiracy theorist, because he hates the term ("It's not a conspiracy theory if it's true!"), but I would say his worldview reflected what Richard Hofstadter called "the paranoid style in American politics." Everywhere he saw malevolent, all-powerful forces shafting the common man. Since my view is that human history is driven by a combination of greed and incompetence, both of which make conspiracies impossible, we would debate for hours about the Federal Reserve, the gold standard, the assassination of Kennedy, 9/11, and so on.

"Why do these issues get you so riled up?" I'd often ask Joey. "Even if you're right—which I don't think you are—you can't do anything about them."

"I don't like people pissing on my feet and telling me it's raining."

Having spent the entire afternoon and evening pissing, I said to Joey, "You will love this gift, but you will hate me for giving it."

Joey opened the bag and pulled out the tinfoil cap with its tinfoil antennas. One look and he doubled over and nearly fell off his chair laughing.

"I do love it, you bastard," Joey said between spasms of hilarity. "It's the best gift ever. I love it. You son of a bitch."

CHAPTER 18
Fight Camp

"Sleep" was the answer Forrest Griffin gave me when I asked him to name the most important aspect of a training camp. As proof of his devotion to the Sandman, Forrest offered that while he does drink eight cappuccinos a day, he never has one after 4 P.M.

In the first two weeks of my training camp, I was sleeping twelve hours a day. It was like I was an infant again. I slept, I ate, I shat, and I cried a lot. Finally Joey pulled me aside and said, "You're a wreck. How's your diet?"

"Good," I lied.

"Then we should get you checked out and start taking some

supplements. They're like healthy steroids, only they won't shrink your nuts."

I was skeptical. To me, supplements were the snake oil of MMA. Fighters swear by them, often spending as much as five hundred dollars a month, but fighters are a superstitious bunch. If you tell them that drinking their own pee will make them a champion, they will do it (e.g., Lyoto Machida).

The supplements guy at the gym was called Dr. John. He had designed Randy's Xtreme Couture brand of athletic pharmaceuticals, worked out of his house, and took only cash. He was built like a former college athlete but was a salesman underneath the muscles. After giving me his pitch and taking some of my money, Dr. John sent me off to get a blood test, so he could analyze the results and prescribe the correct correctives. A week later I returned to hear the bad news.

"You are much worse than the average person I see," Dr. John said, starting strong. "You've got several major performance disenhancers that are killing your cardio. The typical fighter has at most one. You're anemic. Your blood is too thick. Your iron levels are through the roof. You're aging faster than you should be. Your vitamin D level is so low that you have a much greater risk of cancer. And you've got the testosterone count of a thirteen-year-old girl."

That last one stung.

"So I'm guessing I'll need to buy a lot of supplements," I said.

"You should thank Joey for making you do this," John answered without answering. "He may very well have saved your life."

Saving my life cost me four hundred dollars a month and included but was not limited to B12 Nitro, Zinc Clutch, Vita D, AA Resveratrol Blast, Adrenal Glandular, IGF Blast, Natural Mins, Xtra

EnZymes, and O2 Plus+. He printed up a schedule of pill popping that would have choked a horse and made Rush Limbaugh blush.

Em came to visit for a week just as I got the shoebox full of various bottles and the schedule of seventy pills per day. When she saw all the assortment of pill bottles, she burst out laughing.

"My grandfather doesn't take that many and he's ninety-seven," she snickered. "Maybe he can loan you one of his daily pillbox organizers."

It took three days and then it all of a sudden hit me. It was like I had snorted several lines of pure vitality. It is hard to estimate, but it felt like my energy level had increased by fifty percent. The change was so dramatic that I might not have believed it myself if Em hadn't been there as a witness.

Instead of coming back from practice that third day hunched over with exhaustion, I sang and danced my way into the room.

"Honey, what has gotten into you?" Em asked.

I picked up Em, swung her around, tossed her on the bed, and jumped on top of her.

"About two hundred and ten pills."

"Go, go, pharmacology!"

■ ■ ■

MMA fighters generally have two nicknames: an official one and a "gym nickname." Used for promotional purposes, the official nickname is usually powerful and dangerous like The Lion, Sledgehammer, or Hand Grenade. The gym nickname is used only by teammates within the safe zone of the gym and is usually mocking. Harold "The Tiger" Evans might be better known by teammates as "The Dirty Rabbit" because every time he gets kicked hard in the leg in practice he hops around cursing.

It is considered bad luck to pick your own official nickname. Someone else has to give it to you. The story of how and why becomes part of your legend. It is a coming-of-age, entering-the-tribe rite of passage. And it's crucial. A badass nickname that closely matches a fighter's personality, style, or physique can stick in the public's mind. Chuck "The Iceman" Liddell was given his nickname because he never got nervous before fights. When Quinton "Rampage" Jackson fought in Japan, he became famous for flipping out and body slamming his opponents. Cris "Cyborg" Santos is unstoppable in the cage and built like Arnold Schwarzenegger's Brazilian cousin.

On the other hand, an unfortunate nickname opens up a fighter to easy derision from snarky bloggers and MMA trolls. Whenever Peter "The Dutch Lumberjack" Aerts finds himself in the north-south position, the blogs explode with riffs about a similar-sounding deviant sexual act (NSFW: "The Dutch Blindfold"). Vladimir "The Janitor" Matyushenko gets burned after every loss with cracks about the Eastern European immigrant's future job prospects. But sometimes the best way to beat the trolls is to own the joke, as is the case with the brilliantly nicknamed Rick "The Horror" Story.

I couldn't pick my own nickname, but I didn't have time to receive one naturally. With only a few weeks left before my first and last MMA fight, I asked several of my cleverest friends to submit suggestions. Coming up with an MMA nickname is harder than it seems. The only decent suggestion came from Ben Fowlkes, *Sports Illustrated*'s MMA columnist: "The Scholar of Slaughter." It was funny and had the advantage of alliteration, but it wasn't quite right.

Once again Joey came to my rescue. "I woke up this morning

and knew what it should be," he informed me when I arrived at the gym.

"What?" I asked excitedly. Whenever Joey arose with the answer to a question, it was invariably the right one.

"Matt 'American Shaolin' Polly," Joey said.

"I suppose I've earned the right to that nickname."

"The right? Hell, you've got the copyright," Joey laughed. "And you might sell a few more copies of your first book."

"Done, perfect," I said, hugging him. "You're a marketing genius."

I didn't get my gym nickname until three days before my fight. After weeks of enduring a no-sugar, no-carb, no-salt diet, Joey caught me hunched over a Handi-Snacks box of Ritz Crackers 'n Cheez I had hidden in my gym bag. After a dressing down worthy of an army drill sergeant, Joey bestowed upon me my gym name: Matt "Want a Cracker" Polly.

I didn't hug him.

■ ■ ■

"Maintaining a stable emotional life is part of your training," Joey told me early on. He knew I was lonely living in Vegas away from my friends and Em. Before the final weeks of my training camp, he insisted that I come out and hang with his friends every Saturday night.

One of my favorites of Joey's friends was pro fighter Dennis Davis. A scrappy, hard-charging, fearless lightweight (155 pounds), Dennis had already fought most of the top names in the division, establishing himself as a "gatekeeper"—if you wanted to prove you were elite, you had to beat him. A longtime acolyte of Randy Couture, he had the same soft-spoken, even temper, and he was as skilled with the ladies as his master. In a gym filled with playboys, Dennis was the leading light. "He's not much to look at, but the women love him," Joey told me. Dennis had so much action that he'd often come into the gym and try to recruit other fighters to lessen his burden. He was a one-man sexual welcoming committee to Sin City.

"I've got a four set of bachelorettes from Texas on Thursday," Dennis would pitch a fellow team member. "You free? No? Well, I've got a five set from Virginia on Saturday. How about then?"

After several months of listening to Dennis, I finally confronted him. "Obviously, it is too late for me. I'm already bought and paid for. But for my younger male readers, perhaps you could share some of your wisdom as an expert swordsman."

Dennis considered this for several minutes as he walked around the gym, talking to other pros about their evening plans. Finally, he came back to me with a certain resignation, like someone sentenced to fifty hours of community service.

"Fine," Dennis sighed. "I agree to teach you one technique."

"Go on."

"It's called 'The Bounce,'" Dennis started, slowly warming to his subject. "On a first date, most guys think up something elaborate, but at the end of the night it is still a first date and women have rules about first dates. Instead, I invite a girl out for coffee or something. Then I text some friends and arrange to go over to a bar and get some drinks. An hour later, I propose that she and I grab a bite to eat. Bounce, bounce, bounce. It's not a first date; it's three mini-dates. Women have different rules after a third date."

"You're an evil genius," I said with admiration.

"Thank you."

■ ■ ■

In the beginning the only way to get into the UFC was to find someone who was currently fighting in the UFC and join his team. If you did well enough, the senior fighter—Ken Shamrock and Pat Miletich were two early exemplars—would talk you up to the UFC brass, get you a contract, and corner you for your match. As older fighters retired, they opened proper gyms and served as manager/coaches for younger prospects.

But former fighters are not always the best negotiators. So as the sport became more popular and new promotions arose to compete with the UFC for talent, the agent/manager/hustler entered the arena. (Dana White got his start as Chuck Liddell's and Tito Ortiz's manager.) Along with working out the contractual details, the manager also dealt with the growing number of sponsors who were attracted to the sport.

These were not traditional sport sponsors—MMA was still too controversial in the early days—but new apparel companies like TapouT and Affliction discovered a large untapped market in the young men who followed the sport and had an interest in being viewed as tough guys. These guys already had the biceps and the tattoos. By adding an Affliction T-shirt they were declaring to other dudes "I'm into MMA; don't mess with me," and they were signaling to the gals who are into such dudes "I can protect you." What is it worth to the young American male to be able to scare off other dudes and attract big-breasted females? About sixty or seventy dollars for a two-dollar T-shirt with some skulls and bones printed on it in China—a lucrative market with huge margins. At MMA events there were so many of these couples—him with his muscles popping his Affliction tee and her jiggling on top of plat-form shoes—that they became known as the "Tits 'n' Tats" crowd.

The result for the sport was that nouveau riche MMA apparel companies had bucketloads of money to throw at top MMA stars. Wearing a certain company's T-shirt, baseball cap, and shorts into the ring and putting it back on after the match could get you paid as much or more than the fight itself. Given how little many of these promotions, including the UFC, were paying back in the day, sponsorship could be the difference between training full-time or having to work as a bouncer between classes. A smart manager became a crucial asset.

I wanted to experience the entire MMA lifestyle, so I needed a manager and a sponsor. Needless to say, your average, no-name amateur fighter with zero contests can't expect Affliction to show up on his doorstep with a wheelbarrow full of cash. Even fairly established pros often have to make due with dodgy sponsors. (Funniest example: CondomDepot.com stitched their logos across the backsides of the shorts of several popular UFC fighters before Dana White finally banned them.) My only possible pitch was that I was writing a book about MMA and could offer free adver-tising.

I asked around Xtreme Couture about finding a manager who would take me on as a publicity stunt. There wouldn't be any money in it. The best I could expect from a sponsor is that they might send me some free swag. After several days, Nik Fekete, from whom I had taken some private lessons in wrestling, introduced me to Randel Aleman, a twenty-two-year-old former wrestler at Arizona State. Randel's claim to fame was that his father had been the high school wrestling coach of Gray Maynard, one of the top two MMA lightweights in the world, and Gray treated Randel like an ornery little brother.

"How much do managers make?" I asked out of curiosity.

"The maximum the law allows is thirty-three percent," Randel said. "But I believe it should be ten percent for the fight purse and ten percent for the sponsors. My dad taught me never to screw a guy when giving a little extra can result in a long-term relationship."

"Well, let's see what you can do, Randel," I said without much hope.

Miraculously, Randel called me the next week: "I heard back from Everlast. They are interested in doing something."

"You're shitting me? Everlast?" I exclaimed, utterly amazed. Everlast is the oldest and most prestigious equipment company in combat sports.

The next day I phoned Matt Cowan, the Everlast marketing executive responsible for MMA relations.

"Tell me about Everlast," I said, in my softball-tossing voice.

"Our company is about heritage. Everlast is a hundred years old," Cowan said. "We are the most established brand in boxing. We own that space. And we consider it a badge of honor that we sponsored Ali, Frazier, and Tyson."

"What do you look for when you consider sponsoring a fighter?" I asked, hoping he'd mention pudgy writers.

"We want brand endorsers," Cowan said. "Fighters who will match our brand ethos: strength, dedication, authenticity, and individualism."

"So which MMA fighters do you sponsor?" I asked.

"We have a long-term relationship with Randy Couture," he said.

"Because like your company, he's old, reliable, and respected?"

"I might phrase it slightly differently, but yes," Cowan said. "Randy truly believes in the product. He tests the equipment. We put his likeness on our packaging."

"Who else?"

"We've had Gray Maynard under contract for a long time," Cowan said. "And we recently signed Jay Hieron."

"That's it? Three MMA fighters?" I asked, as I thought, *Oh, Gray Maynard, that's how Randel pulled this deal off.*

"We'd rather have a powerful and meaningful relationship with a few guys," Cowan said. "Sign them up as brand ambassadors for two years."

"So how does the brand ambassador gig work?"

"Contracts are generally for a certain number of fights or a period of time: six fights or two years. There is a base pay for exposure at the press conference, weigh-ins, and the event. We expect head-to-toe exclusivity: cap, shirt, shorts, corner signage. There's a kicker if the fight is broadcast on TV. And there is another kicker if they win and wear our clothing when the decision is announced."

"Ah, so that's why sweaty, exhausted MMA fighters are always struggling to get back into their T-shirts before the scorecards are read."

"Right. And we expect our fighters to wear Everlast at public workouts, etc."

"Okay, but to get back to the three fighters," I said. "Aren't you worried that as MMA is slowly surpassing boxing, you're brand will be left behind?"

"I'd dispute that boxing is being surpassed. But we've been around for a long time," Cowan said. "Right now, MMA is the wild west for sponsorship. These MMA T-shirt companies are like dot-com companies used to be, throwing ridiculous money around. Most are going to go bust, and we'll still be here."

The Everlast box arrived for me at Xtreme Couture two days before my fight. I opened it like a kid on Christmas. It was a sweet swag bag: Everlast T-shirts and shorts, boxing gloves, MMA gloves, shin guards, and head gear. The marketing department of a company like Everlast has this stuff just lying around, but at retail prices it was probably worth five hundred dollars. I already had all the equipment and didn't need backups, so I gave most of it away to some of the amateur fighters I knew were struggling to pay for gear. But I proudly put on my Everlast T-shirt and board shorts.

As I walked out, Gray Maynard was standing next to the front desk.

"Gray," I hailed him as if we were old buddies. "Your boy Randel hooked me up with Everlast."

"I heard." Gray turned and smiled at me.

"So now we are fellow Everlast ambassadors."

"I feel better already."

"First they signed Randy, but really who is he, then it was you, but I won't say anything bad to your face, then Jay, who is all right, but finally Everlast came to their senses and put down the big bucks to add me to the team."

"They just keep signing better and better fighters," Gray laughed. "What's your MMA record again?"

"Just like yours, it's perfect," I said. "No losses."

■ ■ ■

Six weeks before my fight I was stuck at 205 pounds, right where I'd been for the previous two months of hard training. When I started at Xtreme I weighed 215—down from 250 when I began this project. Joey's training camp had quickly gotten me to 205, but there I remained. I asked Jake Bonacci, my strength and conditioning coach, what the problem was.

"It's what you're eating," he said.

"Yeah, but I've been training harder and harder and still can't get below 205."

"Working out will only take you so far, the rest depends on diet," Jake said. "I see you in the gym with a can of Coke in your hand. What other kinds of crap are you consuming?"

"Jake, it's not my fault," I mewled. "There's an In-N-Out Burger right next to where I'm living. And there's this Long John Silver's in the other direction. You can get a two-chicken plank meal for $4.99 and all the free crumbs you can eat. Free crumbs, Jake, pure batter-fried yumminess."

"Hey, it's your fucking fight, man." Jake shrugged in his gruff way, pretending like he didn't care.

MMA fighters spend more time obsessing about their weight than high school cheerleaders. That is because they are constantly trying to manipulate it between three numbers: walking weight, weigh-in weight, and rebound weight. "Walking weight" is how heavy they are when they are not dieting for an upcoming fight. "Weigh-in weight" is what they cut down to for the weigh-ins to meet the limit of their weight class. "Rebound weight" is what they bounce back to in the twenty-four hours between the weigh-ins and the actual fight.

Because size gives you a significant advantage when grappling, the goal is to cut as much weight as possible and then rebound as much as possible to come into a match heavier than your opponent. The flip side is if you cut or rebound too much it can exhaust the body, defeating the purpose of gaining a size advantage.

My walking weight was 205. I needed to cut twenty pounds to get to middleweight. I had six weeks. For a professional MMA fighter used to regularly yo-yoing his body mass, twenty pounds is nothing. Many cut from thirty to forty pounds for a fight. This being my first time, I was nervous. If I couldn't get down to 185, I'd have to fight at 205, and I'd be crushed.

As always, Joey soothed my anxieties. "I've got a diet for you. It's going to be an easy, gentle cut."

The underlying principle of Joey's MMA diet was to eat six small meals a day instead of three larger ones. The idea is to keep the metabolism running all day instead of starting and stopping. That way even if you are consuming a similar number of calories, the body will burn up more of them. "Grazing" can also help regulate blood sugar, control cravings, and keep hunger at bay.

The key, however, is to carefully regulate the caloric intake of each meal and slowly decrease it over time. This requires careful, almost tedious planning and preparation. The secret to the six-meal diet may be the number of calories it requires to implement.

Each morning I woke up to find the daily schedule Joey had e-mailed me. A typical example:

Matt (Wednesday)
Drink lots of water, water, water today
You can have pepper and/or mustard but no salt with food
9:00 A.M.: Wake up
9:15 A.M.: Oatmeal with one spoon of peanut butter and one
    of honey
10:00 A.M.: Striking class

11:00 A.M.: Protein shake and banana

12:00 P.M.: Sparring class

1:00 P.M.: Turkey sandwich on whole grain bread and
handful of spinach

2:30–3:30 P.M.: Nap

4:00 P.M.: Two boiled egg whites, no yoke, and apple

5:30 P.M.: Jiu-jitsu class

6:30 P.M.: Protein shake and banana

8:00 P.M.: Chicken breast, brown rice, and broccoli

Joey started me on the diet three weeks out, and I consistently lost about half a pound every day. With one week left, I was down to 194 pounds. Joey switched me to the "equilibrium" phase of weight cutting, which involved removing carbohydrates and sodium. I was flushing my system with two gallons of water a day. In the last two, he switched me to distilled water, which lacks the salt and other chemicals of regular water.

Every night I would weigh myself and Joey would predict how much I should weigh the next morning. He was invariably correct. The few times he was off, he would look at me funny. "Did you eat anything extra last night?"

"No, Coach," I'd lie. I loved those damn crackers.

The day of the weigh-ins, my body was a funnel. Water I poured into my mouth was peed out. My weight was 187.

I went to Xtreme Couture in the morning for the final part of the cut. With so many chemicals removed from my body, I felt autistic. I registered emotions but I felt nothing myself.

I went into one of the private offices with Ryan Couture, who was the headliner on our fight card. He had a can of Albolene—a makeup remover that is used to open the pores to cut water weight.

We sluiced it over our bodies and put on sauna suits, which are glorified garbage bags. Ryan and I went out to the treadmills and started slowly walking.

After about five minutes, the sweat began to pour out of me like a broken dam. Joey had told me to walk for twenty minutes. I was so nervous I wouldn't make weight that I went for forty.

When I pulled off the sauna suit and weighed myself, I was 184 pounds. When I turned around, Ryan was staring at me.

"Hey, look at you, Polly." Ryan smirked. "You've finally got an ab."

■ ■ ■

To have a successful fight career you don't have to be the baddest dude on the planet. You simply have to be better than your next opponent. Early in a fighter's career it is his coach who sets up his fights. A savvy coach builds up his fighter with opponents who are a challenge but not too challenging—"credible but manageable."

"Tuff-N-Uff has picked an opponent for you," Joey told me seven weeks before my fight.

"Who is he?"

"Let's watch the tape."

"He's already fought once?" I asked. "I'm a virgin."

Joey pulled up the YouTube clip of my opponent, Craig, who was facing Tim, an Xtreme Couture teammate of mine. Tim was a former college wrestler, who was younger, bigger, stronger, and much meaner than me. The first time we were paired up together in MMA class, he threw me to the ground so hard he nearly cracked my ribs. After that I went to great lengths to avoid being partnered with Tim.

"They're light heavyweights," I protested. "I'm fighting a middleweight."

"I know," Joey said. "The promoters say Craig intends to drop a weight class."

As I watched the video, my heart sank. In the first round, Craig quickly took Tim down and grounded and pounded him for the entire first round. In the second, Craig continued to dominate until he ran out of gas. When Craig sputtered to a stop, Tim jumped on him and battered away until the referee intervened.

"What do you think?" Joey asked.

"His cardio sucks."

"What do you think of the matchup?"

What I thought was that it was awful. For a round, he had dominated a guy I knew was better than me.

What I said was, "I will fight anyone you put in front of me, Coach."

"Good answer."

Joey immediately changed up my training. He asked Pat Begin to serve as my training partner and proxy for Craig. Pat was a big, broad-shouldered light heavyweight who had wrestled in high school and taught several of Xtreme Couture's beginning jiu-jitsu classes. He had just switched over to MMA and had a couple of amateur fights under his belt. I liked him a great deal, although he did freak me out once.

"There is so much freedom in the cage," he happily told me one day. "Did you know that if you kill your opponent, it's the referee's fault?"

"Ah, no, no, I can't say I did."

"It's just so freeing to know that."

"That's great, Pat," I said, backing away slowly. "So I'll see you tomorrow, my good friend."

After weeks of Pat clinching, throwing, and pinning me to the mat, it was a great relief when Joey pulled me aside ten days before my match to say, "I've got some good news. I got you a different opponent."

"What happened to Craig?"

"He called the promoters and told them he wasn't going to be able to make 185," Joey said. "I knew this was going to happen. I asked around and heard that he barely made 205 last time."

"You had me matched against a collegiate-level wrestler who could barely make the weight class above me?"

"I was never going to let you fight him," Joey said. "It was a terrible matchup for you. But now that he can't make weight, we can honorably refuse the matchup, and we are in a stronger negotiating position with the promoters. They found you a striker without any previous MMA fights."

The word *striker* was exactly what I wanted to hear. After all this training in ground fighting, I could defend myself on the mat. But I wasn't going to win a match by tapping someone out—my best bet was to keep the fight standing and utilize my greater experience in punching and kicking.

"Who is it?"

"His name is David Cexton."

"What's his background?"

"On his fighter application to Tuff-N-Uff, he wrote that he has two years of kickboxing, one year of jiu-jitsu, and one year of aikido."

"He really put down aikido?" I asked. "Which gym does he train at?"

"It says he trains at Nellis Air Force Base," Joey said.

"Great, I'm going to be fighting Maverick from *Top Gun*."

"I doubt he's a fighter pilot," Joey said. "I'll look him up and see what I can find out."

A few days later, Joey said, "I tried to friend him on Facebook, but he turned me down."

"At least we know he's not stupid," I said. "And he knows he's fighting someone from Xtreme Couture."

"Yeah, so I had Lulu friend him and he accepted."

"That'd be a difficult request to reject," I laughed. Lulu was Joey's stunningly beautiful Brazilian girlfriend, who worked as a model for fitness magazines.

"So I poked around and spent two hours clicking through pictures of his friends and their pages," Joey said. "Surprising how much you can learn about someone from his friends."

"What's your assessment?"

"He's young, twenty-three, pretty buff," Joey said. "But he seems a little uncertain of himself. Like you used to be before you went to China."

"Was that necessary?"

"You always hurt the ones you love."

CHAPTER 19
Weigh-ins

———————

"You can't think about victory or defeat in the ring.
Or what anyone else will think of you if you lose.
Your friends, your family, they loved you before
the fight. They will love you after—win or lose. And
everyone else, they don't have the balls to step
into the ring. Just stepping into the ring shows
you are brave in ways they will never be."

—JAY HIERON, MMA FIGHTER

Joey and I walked into the Orleans Casino together. It was my favorite casino in Vegas, because it gave me hope. Interacting with the dealers, the hostesses, and the bartenders, I realized that no matter how bad things might get, I could always get a job at the Orleans. Not since Enron has there been an organization that has employed more misfits, incompetents, and nutjobs than the Orleans. Also I had unbelievable luck at its blackjack tables:

After six months, I was up three hundred dollars, a statistical miracle.

I was lugging my gear bag with all my equipment and a post-weigh-in cooler filled with crackers, cheese, a turkey sandwich, water, Gatorade, and Pedialyte—an electrolyte solution used to replace fluids and minerals that are lost when children have diarrhea. My drop down to 185 pounds, a weight I hadn't known since college, had been relatively smooth. But the moments before and after weigh-ins were the most fraught for MMA fighters. I felt slow, sloggy, wobbly, and utterly drained of emotion. Fatigue makes cowards of us all, but hunger and dehydration can turn you into a zombie—and not the fast *28 Days Later* kind.

I also was carrying a cup filled with ice to moisten my mouth and hopefully to keep me from passing out. I had reason to worry. It had happened to one of Xtreme Couture's best MMA pro fighters, Mike Pyle, a few months prior. The UFC called him up as a last-minute replacement. He had six days to drop twenty-eight pounds. In the last few hours he was still seven short. His teammates wrapped him in a plastic suit and shoved him into a sauna. Thirty minutes later, he could barely crawl on his own. They carried him to the car and drove to the MGM Grand, where they somehow lost track of him. Pyle wandered into a bathroom, collapsed, and was discovered by security. After doctors pumped him with IV fluids to revive him, he refused to quit, insisting that he be allowed to compete the next day. Everyone at Xtreme who heard the story applauded Mike's courage and then promptly bet against him. We all won.

"Let me carry some of your stuff," Joey said, looking at me with concern.

"No, Coach," I said, trying to walk straight. "I've got it."

"Most fighters, when they go to weigh-ins," Joey said, "have an entourage to carry their equipment."

"But I'm not a fighter, Coach," I said. "I'm a martial artist, right?"

"Ho-ho," Joey laughed. "You're gonna use my words against me, aren't you?"

"That's why they pay me the big bucks."

We entered a smallish conference room already filled with dozens of fighters and trainers. Amateur MMA promoters like to book as many fights as possible on the assumption that each fighter will bring multiple friends and family members who have to buy tickets.

The promoters were announcing various instructions. I couldn't register what was said. The only thing I caught was that I had a series of liability, legal, and personal information forms to fill out.

Filling out those forms was like the high-altitude experiments for the astronauts in *The Right Stuff.* I have no idea what I signed. For all I know, Tuff-N-Uff now owns the rights to my life story and my firstborn son. It took me several minutes to remember my fight nickname was "American Shaolin."

After filling out the forms, I progressed through the tables where medical professionals decided if I was healthy enough to get punched in the face repeatedly. A young, quiet Asian woman took my blood pressure. As she stared long and hard at the dial, I tried to repress a growing sense of panic. My blood pressure had been dangerously high before I started studying MMA two years earlier. I hoped it had improved, but I had not checked it again. After what seemed like an eternity, she checked the okay box and signaled that I should go to the next doctor.

"What was it?" I asked her.

"One eighteen over eighty."

I blew a sigh of relief. Two years before it had been 145/100—proof yet again of another way MMA, the most seemingly brutal sport in the world, had helped to extend my life expectancy.

Next was Dr. Chang, who had examined my nose after I realized it was broken. Joey strolled up as Dr. Chang checked my eyes.

"You gonna give him the five-finger rectal exam?" Joey said. "I liked it when you did it to me."

"My fist is still sore from you," he replied.

After Dr. Chang checked off my form, clearing me to fight, I lined up with the other fighters to have our weight checked. I was still alone, which was a problem because the promoters wanted opponents to weigh in together so in case there was a problem (e.g., one opponent was overweight) it could be settled quickly. Everyone in front of me was already paired up, so I turned and scanned the room, looking for my opponent, David Cexton, hoping I'd be able to identify him based on the photo of him I'd seen on the Tuff-N-Uff Web site.

I couldn't find him and began to panic. In the amateur ranks, one of the biggest pre-fight fears is that your opponent won't show. Apparently, it happens all the time. The guys at Xtreme enjoyed telling me no-show horror stories.

"My opponent came to the weigh-ins, and he showed up fight night," my training partner Pat Begin told me. "I was standing in the back hall waiting to fight next when I looked around and realized I was alone. My chickenshit opponent had put on his clothes, walked out of the building, gotten into his car, and driven home, leaving me there in the arena with my dick in my hands."

For the last two weeks I had been petrified my opponent would be a no-show. I had no backup plan. And all my friends had already booked flights to see my fight.

It's fairly easy to get into a scrap when you are drunk and pissed off and not thinking about the consequences. It is qualitatively different to get into a ring after months or, in my case, two years of sober premeditation. As the date rushes toward you like a runaway train, the low-level anxiety and apprehension can slip into genuine terror as your mind plays out worst-case scenarios.

I wasn't worried so much about injury. Cuts, bruises, and broken bones heal. MMA isn't the Roman Colosseum, despite the UFC's marketing strategy. I was 99.9 percent certain that I'd walk out of the ring, perhaps a little worse for wear, but basically intact. I was most frightened of being shamed or humiliated. I was afraid I'd shuffle to the center of the ring, catch a right hook on the button, and eight seconds later have to face the look of disappointment on Joey's face. I didn't want to let him down or let down any of my other amazing coaches, who had invested their time and talent in me.

As all of this was rolling through my mind, someone tapped me on my shoulder. I turned, expecting it would be David Cexton. It was a young, twentysomething tattooed fighter standing next to his equally young coach.

"Yeah?" I asked.

"*Dude*," the youngster asked me in a mocking tone of voice. "How old are you?"

My fuddled brain paused and then the adrenaline kicked in. Suddenly, I was back on the playground. What should I tell him? If I admitted I was thirty-eight, he and his coach might laugh at me, and then it might get ugly.

What to say? What to say? He'd never believe I was twenty-nine.

"Thirty-three," I said, pulling my shoulder back and cocking my head. "And how old are you, *dude?*"

"Twenty-two."

"Well then, you have a lot of time to learn what you need to learn," I said as I turned away from him.

As I did, my brain was thinking, *That sentence made no sense. Is that the best you could come up with? He mocks you for being old and you counter with some vague existential shit. He's a prick—just turn around and punch him in the face. Sure, they'll kick you out of the competition, but seriously, what a way to go. Okay, let's be reasonable, don't blast him. Suck it up, stand here, and wait.*

As I stood stewing, I finally caught a glimpse of David Cexton. He was just finishing the last of the medical exams. I nodded to him, and he nodded back. He joined me in line. We said hello and shook hands.

Of the many, many ways MMA is nothing like a bar brawl, one of them is having to wait in a queue with your opponent a day before the fight and try to come up with small talk.

"Good to meet you," I said.

"You, too," David replied.

As he had so many times before, Joey saved me. He sidled up to David and introduced himself, subtly bracing David between himself and me.

"I'm Matt's coach, Joey Varner," Joey said. "I teach at Xtreme Couture."

"Good to meet you," David said.

"So I saw on your resume that you study aikido," Joey said with a perfectly straight face.

"I do kickboxing," David answered, sensing the implied diss in the question. He was more clever than I thought he'd be.

"Where do you train?" Joey asked, still straight-faced, just a guy interested in his life.

"I don't have a gym—too expensive," David said. "I train over at Nellis Air Force Base."

"Oh, you're in the air force?"

"No, my wife is."

"So you're a striker?" Joey asked, trying to ascertain his strategy for the fight.

"I have some guys I work with on jiu-jitsu," David said, once again cleverly deflecting Joey's question.

"Good, good for you," Joey said.

"Hey, it's great you took this match," I said, worried he might back out. "I'm honored we'll have the chance to test our skills in the ring."

"Me, too," he said.

"No problems with your weight cut?" I asked. "I'm feeling a little blurry."

"I had to drop nine pounds this week," David said. "It was brutal. I'm not sure I made it."

"How did you do it?" Joey asked. "Stop eating?"

"Friends gave me some advice. Suck on Jolly Ranchers; spit them out. Avoid fast foods."

"I've never heard of the Jolly Ranchers diet before," I said.

"So I read you trained in China," David said. "How was that?"

"Hard to sum up in a sentence," I said. "Cool. Intense."

"I've always wanted to go there."

"You're young. You've got time," I said. "Maybe you can take these two punks behind us with you."

"I'm not sure I'm going to make weight," David fretted, as we both got undressed to our boxer shorts to get on the scale.

"Don't worry," I said, still terrified he might find an excuse to bail. "We'll work something out."

In keeping with Tuff-N-Uff's desire to be the amateur version of a pro show, they had tricked out their weigh-ins to mimic the UFC's crowd pleasers. About a hundred friends, family, and fighters were in the room. A paid announcer trilled the fighters' names as we stepped on the balance scale in front of the video cameras.

"Next we have . . . ," the Tuff-N-Uff announcer shouted as he checked his cheat sheet. "Matthew Polly and David Cexton. Middleweights. 185 pounds."

"First up . . . MAAAATTHEW POOOOOLLY."

I stood in my skivvies as an assistant shifted the weights to 185. The bar dipped low. A slight adjustment was made.

"MAAAAATTHEW POOOOOLLY," the announcer repeated. "One hundred and eighty-four pounds."

I breathed a huge sigh of relief. A week prior I was sure I wouldn't make weight. I stood on the scales and made the MMA fighter pose, spreading out my arms like uprights and flexing as best as I was able.

"Next we have . . . ," the Tuff-N-Uff announcer shouted as he rechecked his cheat sheet. "DAAAAAVID CEXTOOOOON."

Down to his boxers, David stood up on the balance scale. It was already set at 185 pounds. It bounced up the wrong direction. The assistant worked to adjust it. Both Joey and I were leaning forward to see the result. The scale balanced at 189 pounds.

"DAAAAVID CEXTOOOOON," the announcer said, before he looked over and saw the result of the scale. "Um, let's see."

He paused and motioned to Jeff Meyer, one of the Tuff-N-Uff promoters. They whispered to each other.

In professional MMA contests, you are allowed to be one pound over the weight limit. Anything beyond that and you can have another hour to sweat it off and try again. If you can't, your opponent is given the choice of either refusing the match or agreeing to take it, in which case a certain percentage of your purse is forfeited to your opponent.

However, this was an amateur fight, so fifteen percent of a zero-dollar purse was, if my math still serves me, zero dollars, and both Joey and I were still more than a little frightened that David might bolt. So when Jeff Meyer waved off the cameraman and asked us what we wanted to do, we nearly jumped over each other saying, "Take the fight. No problem."

David stepped off the scales, clearly feeling a little embarrassed.

"It's only four pounds, David," I said to him. "It's all good."

Moving from the weigh-in itself, our next station of the cross was the stare-down photo. MMA had picked up boxing's tradition of forcing the two opponents—who are so wobbly from starvation and thirst that they can barely stand—to face each other, raise their fists, and stare hard into each other's eyes. Its purpose is promotional, a marketing tool; its spirit is playground, two boys trying to scare the other with the fierceness of their gaze.

When it was our turn in front of another Tuff-N-Uff cameraman, David and I faced each other. He looked into my eyes and I looked into his, or at least I tried to. The room was fuzzy. As I raised my fists, I realized that after two years of tormenting myself over this moment it had finally arrived. It seemed surreal. I looked at David. He stared intensely at me. The situation suddenly felt so

absurd that the corners of my mouth rose. As David saw me trying not to smile, he grinned and I burst out laughing.

"I'm sorry, David," I apologized. "That was my fault. We can
put that in the blooper reel. Let me try again."

On the second try, we posed and stared and acted fierce. The
photo was clicked.

And we were finally able to get a drink.

I rushed over to my cooler and pulled out the bottle of Gatorade.

"No, no, no! Not yet," Joey shouted at me. "Drink the Pedialyte first."

It tasted like cough syrup. I choked down about half the bottle
before I started to gag.

"Joey, is that enough?" I asked. "Can I switch to the Gatorade?"

Joey squeezed his eyes tight and shook his head as if to say,
*How did I get stuck with this big baby? Did I do something wrong in
my past life?*

By the time I had finished the bottle, I had a strong desire to be
held and burped. I switched to the Gatorade and chomped away
at the turkey sandwich. I felt like Dickens's Oliver Twist: "Please,
sir, I want some more."

"Let's go," Joey interrupted.

"We're not done yet?" I asked.

"Oh, Matt," Joey said, shaking his head.

My final stop was in the corridor outside the conference room.
Two assistants had set up a handheld camcorder on a tripod to record "fighter interviews." As I waited in line listening to the questions asked to the fighters in front of me, I imagined a parody
version of the Q&A.

Q: What's your martial arts background?

A: Kick ass fu.

Q: What's your strength as a fighter?

A: Kicking ass.

Q: What's your strategy?

A: To kick his ass.

As I leaned against the wall, David joined me. I didn't know what to say to him.

"You get enough to drink?" I asked. "I've got some extra bottles of water."

"No, I'm good," David said. "Thanks."

Awkward silence.

"So you trained with the Shaolin monks?" David said, making clear he had studied up on me.

"Yeah, two years."

"That's pretty awesome."

Awkward silence.

I noticed a young blonde woman with her arms crossed giving me the evil eye.

"That your wife?"

"Yeah."

"She's beautiful."

"Thanks."

"Next," said the interviewer.

"You want to go first?" I asked David.

"Nah, that's okay. You can."

"Stand against the wall," the interviewer said as he adjusted the camera to get me into frame.

"Your nickname is 'American Shaolin.' Why?" the interviewer asked.

"I trained at the Shaolin Temple and wrote a book about the experience."

"What's your strength?" the interviewer prodded.

"You mean other than my secret Shaolin mind powers? My background is striking," I said, but realizing that David was behind me listening, I didn't want to give away my sprawl-and-brawl strategy so I added, "But I've spent the last two years training with John Danaher at Renzo's Academy and Robert Drysdale in jiu-jitsu. So I feel I have a strong submission game."

"Do you mind showing us a few moves?" the interviewer asked.

I did mind. The advantage of being a rank amateur is that your opponent has no idea what to expect. I didn't want David to pick up anything about my style that he could use. On the other hand, refusing to do it might make it seem like I was frightened. I half-heartedly strung together a few punches and kicks.

"That good enough?" I asked.

"Yeah," said the interviewer.

I walked over to where Joey was standing with a digital camera, discreetly videotaping David's interview.

"What are your strengths?"

"Striking," David said.

"How will you deal with your opponent?" the interviewer asked. "He has such a reach advantage."

If I had bribed the interviewer, he couldn't have asked a more intimidating question.

"I will have to get inside," David said.

"Show us a few moves?"

David threw a left jab, right cross, left hook, and right over-hand. I made a mental note of his last punch, which had some genuine power in it. When you are taller than your opponent, the overhand is the one to fear most.

"What did you think?" I whispered to Joey, because David's wife was a few feet away from us.

"Standard boxing, but a little sloppy," Joey said. "Good power in the right, though. You'll need to keep your hands up."

With the promotional requirements completed, Joey and I turned to David and his wife, who was sizing me up for a shallow grave.

"Hi, I'm Joey Varner," Joey said to David's wife, offering his hand. "I'm Matthew's coach."

"Good to meet you," she said, shaking his hand but still giving me the death-ray glare.

"David says you are in the air force," Joey said, trying to distract her. "Thank you for your service."

That devious bit of praise shook her like a left hook to the button. "Um, you're welcome," she said, briefly breaking visual contact with me to look at Joey. "Yes."

Then she quickly returned to staring at me.

It was a look of such hatred—like she intended to rip out my heart and eat it with some fava beans—that for a moment I didn't know what to say. What do you say in such a situation? "Mrs. Cexton, my name is Matthew, and I will be trying my best to hurt your husband tomorrow night"?

I looked around the hallway, hoping something appropriate would hit me. Several half-formed sentences came to mind, all of which were awful. I could feel everyone staring at me.

"Don't worry about your husband," I finally blurted out. "We'll take good care of him."

She briefly faked a smile that showed teeth and then turned her back on me. She grabbed David by the hand and dragged him away.

"What is wrong with you?" Joey asked as they walked away. "'We'll take good care of him?' Are you a complete idiot? We want him worried, but we need him to show up tomorrow."

"I know, I know, Coach," I apologized. "It was a stupid remark. But she spooked me."

"Hey, hey, it's okay," Joey backtracked, as he was so good at doing. "She is the scarier of the two."

"I'm glad I don't have to fight her."

"Do you see how he's walking on the ball of his toes?" Joey asked me as we followed them down the hall. "His heels never touch the ground."

"Yeah," I said, focusing on the moment and not the swirl inside my head.

"He's shook," Joey said. "I could feel his heart pounding and his lips trembling when we were in line for the weigh-ins. Did you notice that?"

"No, I didn't," I said. "My heart was probably pounding too hard."

"I would have worked him over more," Joey said. "But I was afraid if I did he'd be a no-show."

"Thank you for that."

"He's not going to be able to handle the adrenaline dump in the first round. He will rah-rah-rah charge and try to end it quickly. So we keep with the plan. First round, stick and move. Jabs only, stay defensive."

"Keep away from the wild and crazy."

"Exactly," Joey said. "He will be pumped, swinging for the fences."

"Stick and move."

"Then, the second round, you put together combos. Add the right cross to the jab. As for kicks, wait until the middle of the round. If everything is going well, I'll shout out to you to open up. Just like in sparring."

"Just like the smoker."

"Right, remember that feeling. Hold it inside of you," Joey said. "Third round, you knock him out."

"Okay, Coach."

"You've got this," Joey said.

"You think so?"

"If you don't screw it up," Joey said. "Let's go to dinner."

Joey took me to his favorite Thai restaurant. We spent hours talking and debating every subject, anything except the next day. He nearly convinced me that the Federal Reserve was behind the Cuban Missile Crisis. (It was actually the X-Men.)

After dinner, in an effort to keep me from "spending the night stressing," Joey and I watched *Inglourious Basterds*. While I have been for years a Tarantino fanboy, I must say that as a way to decompress the night before your first MMA fight, there are few better options than watching Jewish soldiers comically slaughter Nazis.

CHAPTER 20
The Sacred and the Profane

<hr>

"Fighting arouses two of the deepest anxieties we contain. There is not only the fear of getting hurt, which is profound in more men than will admit to it, but there is the opposite panic, equally unadmitted, of hurting others."

—NORMAN MAILER

On the drive to the fight, I was worried. This was nothing new. What was odd was that I wasn't worried about myself. I was worried about my opponent, David Cexton. I was afraid I might seriously hurt him. I had spent two years training to hurt someone. I just didn't want to injure him.

As I fretted, a vivid scene kept replaying in my mind's eye: I had David pinned and was pounding away at his face. Blood was everywhere, but he was still coherent and semi-able to intelligently defend himself. I looked over to the ref, but he wouldn't stop the fight. It was a moral dilemma: Would I stop and forfeit the fight or keep punching away?

While contemplating the ethical considerations, I drove past a 7-Eleven, which set off a trigger in my head. Like an alcoholic driving past a bar, I suddenly had an overwhelming desire for orange soda. For weeks, Joey hadn't allowed me to drink anything with carbonation, caffeine, or sugar so I could make weight. Well, I had, I reasoned, so I should be able to have an orange soda. Before I knew it, I'd parked, bought a Big Gulp of Fanta, and was back in the car inhaling like a crackhead. It was the best damn orange soda of my life.

When I arrived at the Orleans, the first thing I did was make sure David hadn't jilted me at the altar. The promoters kept opponents and their coaches in two separate rooms. I peeked into David's, caught a glimpse of him in profile, and sneaked away before he could turn and see me. I wanted him to worry if I had shown up.

And it was a significant worry. Of the twenty-plus matches scheduled for the night, at least four were a bust because of no-shows. I found one of my Xtreme Couture teammates slumped against a wall, nearly in tears, paging through his text messages.

"Your guy bailed?" I asked.

"Yeah, the pussy. And the promoters can't find a last-minute replacement," he moaned. "I've got thirty friends and family here. Half of them flew in from Texas. I'll never get them all back here to see me again."

I sympathized. When they learned of my fight, all my friends and family wanted to come out. It was like a graduation ceremony meets an execution. Initially I resisted. If I lost, it'd be much harder to lie and say I'd won if they were in attendance. Then I found out Tuff-N-Uff posts its fights on YouTube, so it'd be useless fibbing about the result. I told my friends they could come but insisted my parents and Em stay away. In case I took a beating, I didn't want them to see it. And if the fight did go south, I had a real concern that my mother would jump into the ring and go mama grizzly on my opponent.

As for my mates, I felt relatively safe, because almost all of their wives had recently given birth. No way they'd want or be able to come. But it turned out the opposite was true. I was their get-out-of-jail-free-and-immediately-go-to-Vegas card. ("I have to support my friend, honey.") When they met for a pre-fight Sin City dinner, they joked about it. "You have a two-month-old," one friend said to another. "I see your two-month-old and raise you a three-week-old."

Our conference room was a scrum, filled with a couple dozen fighters along with their coaches and teammates. Near the door was a closed-captioned TV that would play all the night's fights, so just in case you weren't nervous enough you could watch one of your teammates take a shellacking. Next to it was a paper tacked against the wall listing the order of the upcoming matches. Mine was thirteenth—my lucky number. The event started at seven P.M., so I guessed I wouldn't be up until after nine. I checked my watch. It was six.

Against the walls were four long tables, separated by curtains, for the three main teams—Xtreme Couture, Cobra Kai, and Striking Unlimited—and one for the independents. I went over to the Xtreme Couture section, where Ryan Couture was sitting on the table surrounded by the Xtreme crew—the young prince holding court.

I dropped my equipment bag and waited to be recognized.

"Matt," he finally said, smiling at me. "You made it."

(I had skipped the rules meeting, which had been held at five.)

"Any changes in the rules?" I asked. "Please tell me they've reintroduced head butts and groin strikes."

"No, alas, but they did say any fighter skipping a future rules meeting would be banned from all future Tuff-N-Uff events," he said. "And I thought, 'Polly could give a shit about that.'"

"One and done, baby."

Joey hadn't arrived and I had three anxiety-filled hours to kill.

I left the room, walked past the vendors selling their MMA gear, and found the bathroom. Fear was already reaching its fingers around my guts and getting ready to squeeze. I pulled out a copy of *The Economist* and parked myself in one of the stalls. I figured there was no point in running back and forth from the bathroom. I intended to wait until I was literally scared shitless.

My internal evacuation took about an hour and multiple movements. The time wasn't wasted, however. From *The Economist*, I learned that the Middle East was a mess, Africa was a mess, and the war in Afghanistan was a mess. Also, China was kicking economic ass and American politicians refused to seriously confront budget deficits.

When I returned to the conference room, Joey was furious. "Where the fuck were you?" he demanded. "I looked everywhere. You're like a child."

"Sorry, Coach, I was in the bathroom," I said, taking a sip from my Big Gulp.

"Is that water?" Joey asked. "It better be water."

"Yeah . . . no," I said. "It's actually, um, Fanta. But, Coach, I already made weight."

"Would you drink an orange soda before a sparring session?"

"No," I lied, dropping my head in shame. (I would totally drink an orange soda before a sparring session.)

Ever sensitive, Joey immediately switched moods. A coach breaks down his fighter to build him back up. But two hours is too short a turnaround for such a process. Joey didn't want to get me down on myself right before my match."

"It's okay. It's okay," Joey said. "Hey, brother, we're here to have fun. Look around you. This is why you've been training so hard. Tonight is the night. Say it, 'There is no place I'd rather be than right here right now.'"

"There's no place I'd rather be than right here right now."

"That's it, brother. Now relax," Joey said, and then, because he was still pissed, added, "But throw away that fucking soda."

The Nevada State Athletic Commission had two officials in attendance: a potbellied older white guy and a black guy in his fifties who looked like they could work for the DMV. (Athletic positions are patronage jobs.) They wore bright yellow NSAC shirts and badges attached to their belts to assert their authority. Their job was to watch over the proceedings and monitor as trainers wrapped each fighter's hands to make sure nothing illegal, like brass knuckles, was hidden beneath the tape.

The potbellied white guy came into our room and announced some "clarifications" to the rules. "Does anyone have any questions?" he concluded.

"I have a couple," Mike Pyle said. He was one of Xtreme Couture's top pros and was working that night as an expert commentator for some of the early fights. "Knee strikes to a downed opponent. If the knee is delivered as the opponent is going down and lands after his hands touch the canvas, is that an illegal blow?"

"It is up to the referee to determine intent," the NSAC official said. "If he judges that the blow was unintentional, then there is no foul. If intentional, then he can deduct a point. Any more questions?"

"Yeah," Mike Pyle continued. "What about blows to the back of the head?"

"Again, if the blow is unintentional or if the fighter receiving the blow turned his head into the strike, making it unavoidable, then there is no illegality. Any more questions?"

It amused me that MMA had reached the point that not only acts but also intentions were part of the rules. In the bad old days, rules were added ad hoc depending on the exigencies of television and the minimal sensibilities of the public. Time limits were added after UFC 4, when the final match between Royce Gracie and Dan Severn ran past the three-hour pay-per-view window and paying customers were cut off. Severn was winning, but Royce beat him in the black of pay-per-view night. Customers demanded refunds. The promoters realized that while the concept of no-holds-barred was central to the sport, content was king. Judges were added after UFC 7, when the final (time-limited) match ended without a clear victor and thus in a fan-displeasing draw. Groin shots were banned after UFC 12 when Kazuo Takahashi ripped off Wallid Ismail's cup and then delivered a punch and a knee to his unprotected family jewels.

By the time I got to the ring, the list of rules had swelled to thirty-one in total.

All in all, it was a long and winding road to the present day, when fighters are, thankfully, much safer and MMA fans have what all sports fans love: an opportunity to argue about the rules.

I was scribbling down some of these thoughts about the rules in a notebook when Mike Pyle walked over to me.

"You're the one doing the book, right?" he asked.

"Yeah," I said. "Sorry, I haven't had a chance to talk to you earlier. But you always seemed busy, and I didn't want to be a bother. And I was training for my fight tonight."

"You're fighting tonight?" Mike asked, surprised. "I thought you were just writing a book. Cool. Good luck."

Mike stood there expectantly, waiting for me to interview him. One of the best things about MMA fighters is that most of them were extremely open and approachable. Unlike football or basketball, the sport was so new that the pros needed to actively cultivate fans and reporters.

"You know, it's funny," I said, "but everyone at the gym seems to have their own Mike Pyle story."

(While all the pros at Xtreme Couture went hard during sparring classes, no one went harder than Mike Pyle. If he hurt you, he didn't let up; he'd just keep going after that injury until the round was up or you couldn't continue. He was like the Marquis de Sade of Xtreme Couture. It seemed like everyone at Xtreme had an injury-related Mike Pyle story. My favorite was Joey Varner's: "He trapped me against the cage with my arm seat-belted behind my back in the first minute of the round and then he kept punching me in the face for the next four minutes. He wouldn't tap me out. He wouldn't allow me to improve my position. He just slowly and methodically pulverized my face for four minutes as I laughed and cried and cursed his mother.")

"I hope they are good stories," Mike Pyle said, somewhat nervously.

"They certainly make an impression," I said. Mike Pyle was the reason I never took a pro class. I was terrified he'd injure me and I wouldn't be able to make this fight.

"Ah," Mike said, catching my drift. "Well, it's a tough sport. Sometimes people forget. But I'm just a country boy."

I smiled. I grew up with country boys. The more country they were the less they felt the need to mention they were country.

"I hope you don't tell any embarrassing stories about me," Mike said, referring to the time he had passed out before weigh-ins. "I had to lose twenty-eight pounds in six days for that fight."

"It is a good story, Mike," I said. "You took the fight on short notice and sacrificed everything to get into the cage."

While I was talking with Mike, the potbellied white NSAC official entered the room. "Is anyone wearing contact lenses?" he called out in a voice that was practiced to project authority.

I turned and raised my hand. As I looked around the room, I discovered to my dismay that I was the only one with his hand up. Then I noticed Joey standing behind the NSAC official. He was making a throat-slitting gesture with his hand and desperately shaking his head NO!

"You have to take them out!" potbelly shouted at me. "It is against the rules to wear them."

After the official left the room, I collapsed into a chair, despondent. I am Stevie Wonder–blind without my contacts. Joey put his hand on my shoulder.

"You might live in New York, but you still have a lot of Kansas left in you," Joey said, somewhere between amused and annoyed. "'Who is wearing contacts?' 'Oh, me! Me!' What did you think? He was going to give you a cookie?"

"I can't see without my contacts, Coach."

"I know."

"I can't fight if I can't see."

"Obviously."

"What the fuck? Wearing contacts wasn't against the rules before."

"Someone in an earlier fight was hit in the eye and hurt and the doctors said the lens scratched his eye."

"Coach, you've got to talk to somebody."

"I will."

"Two fucking years I've spent being tortured. And it all comes down to this moment—"

"Matt—"

"I've already booked my flight home. I can't stay any longer. I left my wife for six months right after our wedding, and she already wants to kill me—"

"Matt—"

"And ten of my buddies flew to Vegas, leaving their babies, to see me in the ring. How am I going to face them?"

"Matt—"

"Coach, I'm going in the fucking ring. If that fat fucker tries to stop me, he's gonna be the first motherfucker I lay out tonight. Because I'm getting in that ring and no one's fuckin' gonna stop me!"

"Matthew Polly, trust me," Joey said, finally breaking through. "Lay down, clear your mind, and remember the strategy. I'll take care of it."

I did trust Joey, totally. His nickname in MMA circles was Joey Vegas because there were few in the Vegas MMA scene he didn't know personally and fewer still he couldn't convince to do what he wanted.

After a few minutes of failing to clear my mind and think

about the strategy, Joey came back. "I talked to the doctor in charge," Joey said. "When he points the light into your eyes and asks 'Are you wearing contacts?' you say 'No.' You got that, Kansas? You say 'No.'"

"I got it, Coach. Thank you."

I climbed under one of the tables, lay down, and rested my eyes. After thirty minutes, the older black NSAC official came into the room to call out names for the next few fights.

"Matthew Polly," I heard him say.

I stood up and raised my hand again.

He took one look at me and burst out laughing.

"No fucking way," he guffawed. "You? Really? No fucking way."

His laugh was so infectious that I started laughing as well. Suddenly, the entire idea that I was about to get into the ring seemed absurd.

"Way to boost up our fighter," Mike Pyle said.

That straightened me up. *Our fighter.* Before, I was just another reporter. The fact that I was willing to get into the ring had raised my status.

"I'm sorry, but shit me not. No fucking way," the official said. "I assumed you were a trainer!"

There was nervous laughter from all the coaches and trainers around the room.

"Oh, that's a great way," Mike Pyle said, angrily, "to boost up *our fighter.*"

Xtreme Couture's boxing coach, Gil Martinez, set me on a chair to apply the padding and tape to my hands. No one knows better how to apply the tape than a boxing coach, so the job had fallen to him for the entire Xtreme Couture team.

As Gil prepared my hands, I thought of something Jacob "Stitch" Duran, the UFC's famous cutman, told me. "The wrapping of the hands is like preparing a gladiator for battle."

When Gil was finished, the NSAC official who had mocked me signed my wrappings. His signature was proof that he had watched the process. "Do I look like a fighter now?" I asked him. He shrugged with embarrassment: "I was just surprised, that's all."

Joey and Gil helped me squeeze my wrapped hands into the MMA gloves Tuff-N-Uff provided for every fighter. Joey then took me to a corner to warm up with punches and kicks. After about five minutes, Robert Drysdale, my jiu-jitsu coach, spent a couple of minutes reminding me of grappling defenses off my back: the place we didn't want the fight to go but were afraid it might.

After the warm-up was over, I triple-checked my gloved fists and my (relatively worthless) cup, and then I put in the third and last piece of armor allowed in the MMA ring: my mouth guard. I had always hated them because they slip at inopportune moments and make breathing difficult. But Joey had directed me to Dr. Adam "The Fight Dentist" Persky. He had replaced the boil-and-bite mouthpieces with a retainer-like mouth guard, which fit so perfectly I could barely feel it. More important, he offered any design you wanted. I chose Buddhist monk orange with the word "Shaolin" written across the front in black. Most important, his guard helped to lock my jaw into place, making a knockout less likely. And in my upcoming match I was going to need all the help I could get.

The NSAC official shouted out: "Matthew Polly!"

My heart raced.

It was time to fight.

Two years of training for a maximum of six minutes of fighting, three two-minute rounds.

All that anticipation.

All that pain and effort.

All that sweat, blood, and tears.

All that making Em miserable and promising I'd make it up to her later.

All that for this moment.

CHAPTER 21
Fright Night

"My life is changed now that I have seen. If Polly
can do it, I can do it as well."
—TUFF-N-UFF COLOR COMMENTATOR

Before we walked out of the holding room, Joey went over to Randy Couture and whispered in his ear. Randy nodded, smiled at Joey's entreaty, and stood up to follow us. Among his friends and colleagues, Randy had a reputation for being too kind and generous. This was a case in point. Randy agreed to stand in my corner, despite the fact that we'd had maybe two conversations between us. I was a beginning student at his gym, a scrub amateur, but Joey asked Randy for a favor and he kindly agreed to do me the honor.

And so my cornermen and I left the room. We walked down the hall past the kitchens to wait at one of the doors to the ballroom for the current fight to end and my turn to be called. Around the corner was my opponent, David Cexton, with his wife and his two training partners as his corners. His wife looked at me with her death-ray eyes. Sensing she was making me nervous, Joey went over to shake her hand and say something charming and then patted David on the back before coming back to prep me again.

"What are we going to do?" Joey asked.

"Stick the jab. Slow the fight down. Avoid takedowns."

"Second round?"

"Add combinations."

"And then?"

"Wait for your signal, Coach."

"If things are going well, open with a high kick," Joey said. "And the third?"

"Highlight reel."

"Where would you rather be?"

"No place but right here right now, Coach," I laughed.

"You a gamer?"

"I'm a gamer."

All the fear was gone. I was ecstatic. I stepped back and took a moment to look at my team: the Hall of Famer Randy Couture, the grappling master Robert Drysdale, the charmer Joey Varner, and my stalwart training partner, Pat Begin. Given where I started and how mediocre my talents, the present company made me burst out laughing at the sheer good fortune and absurdity of the situation. The idea when I started two years prior that I'd one day be walking into an MMA fight with Randy Couture was ridiculous.

"What do you think I should do, Randy?" I asked, thinking that this was my last chance to ask a legend for some final wisdom and guidance before the bell rang.

"Keep doing what you are doing," Randy said. "Keep laughing and joking. Keep it loose. You've prepared for this moment. It should be fun."

Having watched every UFC video, I had heard Randy's husky voice so often that for a moment it felt like I was a character inside a UFC DVD. A shiver ran up and down my fanboy spine.

From the crack in the door, we could see the previous fight had ended.

"They are going to want to rush you to the ring," Joey said. "That raises the heart rate. Wait. You ain't on their time; they on yours. Wait. Don't enter until *you* are ready."

The door opened and a Tuff-N-Uff official pointed at me and said, "Now."

Joey put his hand on my chest.

"Where would you rather be?

"No place."

"Than?"

"Right here right now."

"You ready?"

"I'm ready, Coach."

"You're ready, brother," Joey said, removing his hand from my chest. "Now, breathe."

I inhaled, centered myself, and walked through the door.

I took three long strides into the room before stopping cold. The promoters had turned down all the lights and cranked up the smoke machine for my entrance. I couldn't see anything. I put my left hand out and shuffled forward slowly. It was like walking through a haunted house. I was desperately afraid some audience member would stick his foot out and that I'd trip and be laughed out of the arena.

I finally found the light. The ring was lit up like the final scene of *Close Encounters of the Third Kind.*

"Drop down to what you will wear in the fight," an unknown official said to me as I arrived at the edge of the ring.

After taking off my shoes, I slowly removed my Everlast-sponsored T-shirt.*

The doctor, whom Joey had fixed, came up, spread my eyelids, and focused a penlight in my eyes. From the background, I could hear the potbellied NSAC official shouting, "He's the one with contacts!"

"Are you wearing contact lenses?" he asked.

"No, sir," I lied.

"Okay," he said and sagged like a compulsive gambler paying off a late wager.

Stepping into the ring, I noticed the two massive video screens displaying me in detail. As they say, television adds ten pounds. The trunks I was wearing were a gift Joey had given me the day before. He'd ordered black Muay Thai shorts and had sewn on patches from both Xtreme Couture and his own brand, Varner Striking. The problem was that the shorts were a size too small, and the elastic around Muay Thai shorts constricts around the waist. The entire effect was to emphasize and exaggerate my muffin top.

"What do you think of them?" Joey asked, expectantly, when I had first put them on the night before.

---

* The preeminent brand in boxing since 1910, Everlast is a global leader in the design, manufacturing, licensing, and marketing of authentic boxing, mixed martial arts, and fitness-related sporting goods equipment, apparel, footwear, and accessories. (Is that good enough, fellas?)

"I love 'em," I said. "But they are a little tight. Don't you think they make me seem pear-shaped?"

"Maybe that's because you are pear-shaped."

As I looked at myself on the humongous screens surrounding the ring, all I could think was: *My God, everyone can see my back fat.*

I had been called to the ring first—age before beauty. In MMA it was traditional to run or slide step around the ring or cage several times when you first entered. In theory, this was to help a fighter get a sense of the dimensions of the space, since ring and cage sizes can vary greatly. In practice, it was about staying warm, burning off nervous energy, and showing off for the crowd.

I'd had done this before, but this was my first time with a camera crew inside the ring, pulling around long, thick power cords. As I circled I was less focused on the upcoming match than I was on not tripping and falling.

After David entered and circled, the silver-haired ring announcer, who had clearly gone to the Bruce Buffer School of Introductions, stepped forward, consulted his cheat sheet, and over-enunciated: "This is for three two-minute rounds in the one hundred eighty-five–pound division. Once again our referee in charge is Jason Trevino. Introducing first, he'll be fighting out of the red corner and in the ring this evening wearing the black trunks. And he's representing Xtreme COUTUUUUURE. Ladies and gentlemen, here is Maaaattt POOOLLY!!"

"His opponent, across the ring, fighting out of the blue corner. He's wearing black with the red and white flames. And he fights for and represents Nellis Air Force Base. Ladies and gentlemen, please welcome David CEEEXTON!!"

I looked up at one of the big screens as the camera focused on

David. Typical of MMA fighter-fans of his generation he had the prerequisite number of bad mofo tattoos, including a scorpion. What was amazing is that the promoters had found someone even whiter than me. We had both trained in the summer in the Mojave Desert, for God's sake. Could neither of us have gotten some sun? With the intense lighting, our torsos were nearly fluorescent—the unbearable whiteness of being. We must have been two of the palest people to face off since the potato famine.

The referee, Jason Trevino, called us to the center of the ring. He was a pro fighter at Xtreme Couture who had, unlike many others, gone out of his way to be nice to me, complimenting me after the smoker on my improvement. We had bumped into each other in the hallway before the event.

"If my opponent is whaling on me, feel free to stop it early," I joked. "I don't want him to destroy my boyish good looks."

"I'll call it fair," he said, not appreciating the jest. "Just like I would for any other fight."

As opposed to the theatricality of the weigh-in stare-down, the in-ring stare-down is something else entirely. Jacked up on adrenaline and testosterone, it's the last chance for a fighter to gain a psychological edge. The two basic choices are to lean forward and stare with bad intentions into your opponent's eye, or to look away as if to say "You are not worthy of my intensity."

It is a ritual, part of what makes ring combat sacred and not profane. But things can go very wrong. The most infamous example happened in Japan, of course, where their MMA events are as Bizarro World to us as their game shows. Heath Herring, who was popular among Japanese fans largely for wearing a cowboy hat and duster coat to the ring, was staring into the eyes of his opponent, Yoshihiro Nakao. As their foreheads touched, Nakao leaned in and gave Herring a peck on the lips. Heath immediately jerked his head back and delivered a quick right hook to Nakao's button, knocking him out cold. After the ring erupted, Herring retreated to his corner. "He tried to kiss me on the lips like a homosexual," Herring explained to the refs before protesting too much, "I'm not gay. I'm not gay."

I was too amped up to feel amorous. What I felt was curiosity. David had seemed awkward and anxious at the weigh-ins. I wanted to look into his eyes to see if he was ready to fight. I saw no fear, just intensity and singularity of focus.

Good, I thought. *You've come to play.*

No fighter wants to lose. But no fighter wants to face an opponent who is going to run and pray for the judges' scorecards. It's dishonorable and a waste of time and effort (see: Nate Quarry vs. Kalib Starnes, UFC 83).

The referee said something briefly to us, which I assume was something like "I want a good, clean fight. Obey my commands at all times." So intense was my focus, I didn't hear a word he said. As far as my senses were concerned, no one else in the universe existed but David and me.

Watching the video afterward, it was at this point that the announcers really engaged in the proceedings. The commentary team included a jaded play-by-play announcer, an excitable color commentator, and Eddie Bravo serving as expert commentator. Eddie was a jiu-jitsu instructor, author, and musician, who was perhaps best known for being UFC commentator Joe Rogan's BFF. In the world of MMA, this qualified him as royalty.

"All right, here are two guys who just want to have a lot of fun and enjoy themselves," the jaded play-by-play announcer said, engaging in the fine art of lowering expectations. "They train; they work. But how about the *Washington Post* writer putting a book together. . . ."

"That's a great story," the excitable color commentator said. "This guy's a writer for the *Washington Post* and he wrote a book that's on the *New York Times* bestseller list. And he's now inside the Tuff-N-Uff ring touching gloves."

"And coincidentally, he's built like the baddest man on the planet, Fedor Emelienenko," Eddie Bravo joked, making fun of our mutual pear-shaped bodies.

"You wonder what Polly will say after the fight," the play-by-play announcer said. (Oh, if he were petty, he might say something about the *Scanners*-like mind-blowing quality of Eddie Bravo's music. But he prefers to take the high road.)

After the referee's instructions, David and I returned to our corners. The bell rang and we shuffled toward the center of the ring. The tradition is to touch gloves, step back, and start fighting. But guys have used this opportunity for a legal but unsportsman-like sucker punch. While tapping gloves is a tradition, "protect yourself at all times" is a *Million Dollar Baby* maxim. So to keep safe, I raised my shoulder, tucked my chin, and pointed out my arm at a forty-five-degree upward angle—somewhere between a Black Power and a Nazi salute. Without incident, David tapped my glove, and we stepped back and started fighting.

I circled as David came forward. I tossed out a few jabs to keep him at bay. David opened with a leg kick. In my mind, I saw it coming from a mile away. *Here comes the leg kick. It's about here. And it landed. That's going to hurt tomorrow. How did you not check that kick? You idiot! You always check that kick. Dammit, now you've let him score the first blow of the match.*

Flush with success, David tried the same kick again. After the mental thrashing I'd just given myself, I checked it successfully.

I continued jabbing as David swung and missed with big hooks. I was supposed to keep jabbing but that leg kick was still annoying me, so I broke with the game plan and kicked him in the leg to even the score.

As David stalked me, I circled and jabbed, trying to gauge and time his rhythm. I had become used to quickly picking up the pattern of most traditionally trained MMA fighters, but David's movements were unusual and I was having trouble getting his timing down. He clearly trained in some martial art outside the normal MMA pantheon. Instead of balling his hands into fists, he kept his fingers pointed like spears at my face, which was disconcerting. MMA's open-fingered gloves—necessary for grappling— had resulted in some nasty eye pokes. I had a feeling this was going to be an awkward match.

"Cexton's got a mean look in his face; he's intense. He's got the open hands of the Muay Thai," the color commentator said.

I nailed David with a solid jab, causing him to take a step back and shake the cobwebs out of his head. I knew I had him slightly hurt, so I kept circling and kept jabbing. Pop, pop, pop. I could see that a quarter-size red welt had formed on his forehead. It wasn't big, but it gave me a target. Pop, pop, pop.

"Polly's got a serious jab," Eddie Bravo added. "That jab's insane." (The author would like to amend his previous comment about Eddie Bravo's music and state for the record that Eddie Bravo is a musical genius.)

Frustrated, David changed his stance to southpaw. It was a mistake—very few fighters are talented or experienced enough to fight ambidextrously. I kicked him on his new lead right leg and popped him in the face with a few more jabs for good measure. Frustrated, David switched back to orthodox and started loading up on big right hooks, his money punch. I was able to slip them easily.

"Polly's got a little *Matrix* in him here, a little Neo," the color commentator said. "He chin is way up in the sky, but he's not getting hit by anything."

I couldn't hear a word my corner was saying (I was later told they were screaming, "Keep your hands up!"), let alone the commentators, but I wish the color commentator had knocked on wood or thrown salt over his shoulder after he made that remark. As soon as a commentator says anything that definitive, the exact opposite tends to happen.

And sure enough, just seconds later, David finally caught me with that right hook he'd been trying to land all round. It didn't hit flush, but it scraped across my left eye, ripping out my left contact lens.

I cursed the fates. This wasn't merely bad; it was terrible. I instantly lost all peripheral vision from my left side, which was where all his right hooks were coming from. And I lost all depth perception.

I couldn't ask for a break to put in new contacts, because I'd already lied about wearing them. And I couldn't say anything to the ringside doctor, because no doctor will allow a one-eyed fighter to continue. Whether it is blood dripping into the eye from a cut or swelling from a bruise, as soon as vision in one of the eyes is significantly impaired, the fight almost always gets stopped.

Any advantages I might have had in terms of experience and quality of training over David had been erased. I was now in real trouble against a younger, faster, bigger, and stronger opponent.

Any empathy I might have had for David before the match went flying out of the ring along with my contact. I needed to finish him and I needed to do it fast.

Moments after knocking out my contact, David caught me on my newly minted blind side with another blistering right hook. This one was on the button.

On the video, you can see that the blow made me stand up straight as a board like a soldier being called to attention. Then I looked over at the referee, which caused the color commentator to say, "Uh-oh, he's looking at the referee like, 'Did you hit me?'"

In my scattered brain, time slowed and the entire arena went black like the lights had been switched off. A bell rang in the distance. I was vaguely aware it was the end of the round. But the room was so dark I couldn't see Joey or my corner. A voice inside my head said, "Put your hand out and walk forward slowly. Before long you will touch the ring ropes. Then turn right and keep walking. A ring is a square. That means it only has four corners, so if you keep turning right you will eventually find your corner."

I felt like Moses wandering in the desert. After what seemed like forty years, I somehow found my corner. Joey had his hands on my face, shouting at me. I couldn't hear what he was saying, but the lights were back up and I could see out of my one good eye again.

On the video, the whole thing took less than two seconds. I looked over at my corner, didn't see Joey, turned 180 degrees and took two steps toward the center of the ring. Noticing my confusion, the referee pointed me back to Joey. I switched back, took three steps, and was being administered by Joey.

"Face me!" Joey shouted, shaking me back to awareness. "Look at me!"

"I can't see out of my left eye," I whined, shaking my head. "My contact got knocked out. I can't see his hook."

"It's all good. It's all good, baby," Joey tried to reassure me. "What did we say about your hands?"

"Keep them up."

"That's right," Joey said. "And now it is even more important than ever. Keep that left hand up. All he's got is the hook."

"It's a good hook."

"You've hurt him."

"He just about fucking knocked me out with it."

"Just keep your hands up."

"What did you think about the first round?"

"It was good. It was good. It was good."

"Did I win the first round?"

"It was good."

My heart sank and my body sagged. In the ring, Joey was Mr. Positive Affirmation. Awesome = great; great = good; good = bad. If he said "good," then he thought I'd lost the round. I was now in a hole with only one good eye. I needed to be perfect for the next two rounds or finish him.

The commentators were more exuberant:

PLAY-BY-PLAY ANNOUNCER: "Polly made it through round one."

COLOR COMMENTATOR: "He *won* round one!"

PLAY-BY-PLAY ANNOUNCER: "All right, Eddie, there were no highlights in that first round, but what did you take from it?"

EDDIE BRAVO: "I thought there were highlights. Polly landed maybe ten, fifteen jabs."

COLOR COMMENTATOR: "Look at the face of Cexton."

PLAY-BY-PLAY ANNOUNCER: "He is stunned. How did he get hit? he's thinking."

COLOR COMMENTATOR: "'How many guys am I fighting out there? Is he shape shifting? Is he using the Buddhist Temple?'"

When the bell rang for the second round, I knew I needed to make an impression. I needed, as Joey had strategized, to open up. As we faced each other, David was no longer chasing me. I could tell he was tired. I opened with a jab followed by a cross that skipped over his head. David countered with a right hook that missed by a country mile.

"Look at the movement by Matt 'Nino' Polly," the color commentator said, mispronouncing the name of Neo from *The Matrix*.

"Polly's stunning Cexton with his moves in the ring," the jaded play-by-play announcer said, slowly switching over to my side.

"Cexton is really intense," the color commentator said. "'How do I hunt this fellow down?'"

David followed me as I circled, instead of cutting off the ring— a sign of exhaustion. I started combining low kicks with high jabs and crosses. I was performing as I had been trained. Combinations: low kicks and high punches. David was finding it difficult to defend attacks from two different levels.

I faked a jab and landed a solid right cross to David's chin. It was my best punch of the night. His entire head snapped around.

"Oh! A big right hand," the play-by-play announcer said.

"A humongous right hand," the color commentator added.

When David faced me again, I could see the hurt in his eyes. It looked like he no longer wanted to be in the ring. I hadn't broken him, but his heart, which wanted victory or defeat with honor, and his brain, which wanted to live to fight another day, were now in conflict. It takes years of training to turn off the brain's survival instinct. I knew if I kept pressing him I might be able to break his will.

I nailed David with a leg kick and followed up with a solid jab, causing him to switch up his stance again. Seeing he was in deep trouble, I went headhunting, swinging rights and lefts wildly at his head, missing most of them.

"Cexton doesn't know whether to go southpaw or orthodox," the color commentator said. "'What kind of strategy am I going to use against a man like this?'"

As soon as the commentator said that, I got caught again. I'd forgotten Phil Nurse's maxim that the most dangerous time is when you have your opponent hurt. As I was pressing forward aggressively, David slipped his right hook past my guard, catching me again on the button and whipping my head around.

"He blindsides Neo!" the play-by-play announcer cried out, speaking more truthfully than he knew.

The room went dark again. Fireflies flickered in front of my eyes, but I couldn't see anything else. He'd hit me so hard I couldn't remember my mother's maiden name. And high school algebra disappeared forever.

Inside my head, I heard Joey's voice shouting, "Circle! Circle! Keep your guard up!"

These are the moments for which all the hard training is intended. Without it I'm sure my knees would have buckled and I would have collapsed to the canvas.

Needing to buy time so my head could clear, I circled. My left leg wasn't responding, and it felt like I was dragging a crippled limb around the ring.

Seeing I was hurt, David went in for the kill, swinging and, fortunately for me, missing with several hard hooks.

"Polly doesn't want another right hand," color commentator said.

The fog finally cleared, the lights turned back on, and my left leg was working again. I felt rejuvenated, suddenly full of energy.

I squared to face David. I kicked toward his thigh. He reached down to grab my leg, leaving his face open. I smacked him with a right cross to the tip of his chin. Shaking his head, David backed off.

The audience started clapping and chanting. My spirits soared. I had won the crowd.

Wanting to give them something they had never seen before in this particular match, I threw a high shin kick to David's head, which landed on the backside of his skull.

I nailed David with another solid leg kick, causing him to switch his stance yet again. I slid to his left, putting his body perpendicular to mine. With him turned at an awkward angle, I blasted him with a right cross that rocked his world.

As Joey would say, you've got crack in that punch, son. As boxers would say, the last thing to go is power. As I would say, the only things you gain with age are wiliness and racism.

Stunned, David turned his back to me.

He's done, I thought to myself. *He wants out.*

You never, ever, while standing, turn your back on your opponent. You can no longer intelligently defend yourself, and after a few more punches the ref is obliged to stop the match. So I knew I needed to hit him a few more times.

Feeling how close to a finish I was, my killer instinct kicked in. I smelled blood in the water. I wanted to end this right here right now. Nothing was going to stop me.

In my head, I punched four, five, six times with my right and left hands trying to get to the side of David's face. But he kept turning his head, frustrating me from getting a clean shot. I briefly considered jumping on his back for a rear naked choke, but I knew there wasn't much time left in the round and I didn't want to risk taking it to the ground. I kept trying to punch him in the face as he ducked and twisted his head back and forth.

On the video, it took less than a second. David had grabbed my right hand to keep me from punching him with it. So with my left I threw two big looping hooks with evil intent. As David moved, the second left landed on the back of his head right before the bell rang. I let go of him and strutted back to my corner.

"Good round," Joey said.

"Great round?" I asked.

"Awesome round!" Joey confirmed, and then continued to talk at me.

I was listening, but I don't remember anything he said. All I remember is that I suddenly felt exhausted after the huge adrenaline surge. I wasn't sure I had a third round left in me. I looked over to Cexton's corner and could see that he was slumped in his stool with the ring doctor pointing a light into his eyes.

On the video, the commentators were going crazy in a way that almost made me want to cut them in on the royalties:

PLAY-BY-PLAY ANNOUNCER: "Round two has come to an end, and the fans are going nuts!"

COLOR COMMENTATOR: "Matt 'Nino' Polly has got to be one of the fastest fighters that I've seen inside the Tuff-N-Uff ring."

PLAY-BY-PLAY ANNOUNCER: "Very deceiving . . . and it's done!"

COLOR COMMENTATOR: "He's done!"

PLAY-BY-PLAY ANNOUNCER: "It's over!"

COLOR COMMENTATOR: "It's over!"

PLAY-BY-PLAY ANNOUNCER: "He got stopped!"

COLOR COMMENTATOR: "He can't take any more of this! He can't take any more of this!"

While the commentators already knew the result, it took about thirty seconds for the message to get to our side of the ring. Few things are more confusing than a doctor stoppage between rounds. The doctor was talking to the ref. The ref was talking to David's corner. Finally, someone started shouting, "It's over! It's over!"

When our corner heard, Joey and the rest were jumping into the air. All I felt was a sense of relief that I didn't have to go out again for another round. And an even bigger sense of relief that after all this time and effort, pain and suffering, it was over. I'd succeeded in what I'd set out to do: train in MMA, fight a match, and win it. Now I could officially retire and return to what I was good at: watching TV and telling jokes.

"Get your hands in the air!" Joey shouted at me. "Look happy!"

I tried. But it was a lackluster effort. At that moment I felt a little empty inside and just wanted to go home.

The most sacred rite of any ring or cage match is its closing.

The fighters meet, shake hands, maybe hug, and say gracious things to each other. It closes the circle, indicating that any violence inside the space has ended there. Like in a courtroom, a judge has presided, a jury has delivered its ruling, and it is final. The conflict has been resolved. The beef has been settled. Society can move on.

I went over to David's corner. His wife, the doctor, and his cornermen had him surrounded. Some winning fighters linger over this moment. Hugging, holding, whispering encouragement or praise in the losing fighter's ear. That has always struck me as slightly patronizing.

I touched David on his knee. He glanced in my direction, but his eyes were glazed and unfocused. I patted him on the shoulder. "Good fight," I said. Then I shook his wife's hand but avoided looking into her eyes, because I didn't want to see what was there. I turned and walked away.

I hugged my cornermen and thanked them. Joey pulled me to one of the sides where the local newspapers were snapping photos. I put my arms around Pat Bergin, Randy Couture, Joey Varner, and Robert Drysdale. The photo made the cover of the sports section for the local Vegas newspapers.

On the video, the commentators went nuts.

"Polly is taking pictures with Randy Couture inside of the ring," the color commentator said. "He's a legend inside the Tuff-N-Uff ring now. Polly is unstoppable. My life is changed now that I've seen. If Polly can do it, I can do it as well."

"He is everyman," the play-by-play announcer said.

"Ladies and gentlemen, at the end of the second round the blue corner retires," the ring announcer said into his mic. "The winner by TKO victory, MAAAATT POOOLLYYYY!"

The very sexy ring girl put the victory medal around my neck. Her name was Stephanie and she worked the front desk at Xtreme Couture. And, as proof that high school never really ends, she was dating Ryan Couture, who was the headliner for the night's event.

"Congratulations, Matt," Stephanie said.

"If things ever don't work out with Ryan . . ."

"Feeling good about the win, are we?" she laughed.

"To the victor the spoils."

With all the excitement in the ring, the surprise and the exhaustion evaporated and the thrill of victory kicked in. It felt like my ego had been turbocharged, and I was walking on air.

Joey picked me up and spun me around. "You did it, brother."

"You did it, Coach," I said. "You saved my life."

"Aw, shucks," Joey laughed. "So how does it feel?"

"Better than any high."

"That's why fighting is so addictive."

As I climbed through the ropes and walked down the steps, the doctor who had falsely testified that I wasn't wearing contacts grabbed my arm.

"You should invest in some fucking Lasik," he hissed.

"My apologies," I said, pulling my arm free. "And in retrospect, I totally agree."

I got halfway down the aisle before I stopped dead in my tracks. There she was, standing in the aisle.

Em.

My wonderful, wicked, sneaky wench of a wife had flown out to Vegas without telling me. I could not have loved her more.

As I approached her, Em looked stunned, as if she had been in the ring fighting beside me.

"Are you okay?" I asked, suddenly worried. "You look upset."

"No, I'm fine," she said. "I just was afraid you'd be angry that I came."

"Not now that I've won."

We hugged again.

"You're sweaty."

"I've been busy," I said. "So what was it like to watch me in the ring?"

"I felt like Michael Phelps's mother," she said. "I had a death grip on your friends' hands and was screaming, 'Hit him! Hit him! Hit him!'"

"And you didn't freak out when he clobbered me?"

"You left me for six months to live in Vegas," Em said. "You deserved a few smacks."

"And that's why I love you," I said. "Your Old Testament sense of justice."

"You should get changed."

"Wait here. I'll be back."

I went looking for David to make sure he was okay. I was concerned. A fight forms a powerful and strange bond between men. I searched high and low but could not find him anywhere. As I was looking, I ran into Joey.

"Have you seen David?" I asked. "I can't find him."

"Have you searched the local hospital?" Joey smiled. "They took him out in a stretcher."

"Oh shit, is he okay?"

"I hear you broke his jaw."

"That's terrible," the angel on my shoulder said, while the devil on the other said, "That's how badass we are! Mess with us and you get your jaw cracked!"

(It wasn't until the next day that I found out that the rumor was untrue. David had simply been dizzy and they took him to get an MRI to make sure there weren't any problems. There weren't. My angel was relieved, my devil annoyed.)

When I walked into my team's room, I was high-fived by all the Xtreme Couture guys.

"That was the best fight of the night!" said Big John, one of the pros and coaches at Xtreme.

"No, it couldn't have been," I said.

"I'm serious! I wouldn't say it if I didn't believe it. He had you in trouble a couple of times and then you rallied. It was great!"

"Well, he knocked out my contact in the first, so I couldn't see his hooks," I blurted out, before realizing I was making excuses. "Anyway, he was tough. He had heavy hands."

As I was changing into my street clothes, another Xtreme teammate came over, gave me a high five and asked, "How does it feel?"

"Like I'm king of the fucking world!" I shouted out, like James Cameron.

Gray Maynard, who was sitting next to where I was changing, laughed in sympathy as if to say *I remember what that felt like, kid*.

I called my mother.

"Matthew!" Mama Polly exclaimed.

"Hey, Mom, well, it didn't go so well," I said, pretending to be glum.

"Don't you tease me!"

"Okay, okay, I won."

She burst into tears: "Don't you ever do this to me again!"

"I promise I'll never tease you again."

"You will never fight again," she continued to cry. "I can't go through this again."

"Dad there?"

"Matthew."

"Hey, Papa Doc."

"I hear you won."

"Yeah, I did. They stopped the fight after the second round."

"You suffer any injuries?"

"Me? No, not really. Got a bruise on my leg from a kick, but it'll go away in a couple of days."

"And the other fellow?"

"I hear I broke his jaw."

"That's terrible," my father said, then he paused to reconsider. "Good for you, son."

The local newspaper reporters covering the event had gotten a whiff that a fellow ink-stained wretch had been on the card and they wanted to interview me. Ryan Couture, as the famous son, was the lead story for the evening, but truth be told they were more interested in mine. Journalists like nothing more than to write about each other. Of course, they misquoted me and threw in a few snarky comments about my plump physique. Never trust a journalist.

I went back out to the ballroom to find Em. As I was looking for her, two cuties rushed over to me.

"Can I get a picture with you?" one of them asked.

"Sure," I said, pleased as punch.

She handed her camera to her friend and snuggled in close. The friend couldn't figure out how to work the camera and as I waited, the cutie started rubbing her hip against my thigh as her cheap perfume stuck in my nostrils.

It occurred to me that it had taken me thirty-eight years to finally acquire my first groupie, and sadly it was too late: I was already married. But it was a good thing my wife was in the arena. The thrill of victory was throbbing through my veins. I hadn't felt this horny since high school. Evolution desperately wanted me to spread my conquering seed.

Why do men fight? I can give you at least one reason.

The friend finally took the picture. The groupie looked up at me expectantly.

"I should go, yeah, I should really go and find my wife," I said, gently pulling out of the bear hug she had around my waist. "It was very nice to meet you."

I finally found Em in the crowd.

"Let's get some chairs in the back and watch Ryan's match," I said.

After it was over (Ryan won in the first round), Vitor Belfort, one of my favorite MMA fighters, walked over in our direction. He gave a thumbs-up and a wave in my direction. Even though I was sitting with my back to the wall, I was so certain that he must have been saying hi to someone else that I actually turned to look over my shoulder before finally realizing he was addressing me.

"Great win," Vitor said with a big smile.

"Aw, well," I demurred. "It was an awkward fight."

"You famous!" he exclaimed, his English still a work in progress.

"Not for that performance, certainly."

"No, you write book, yes?"

"Yes."

"I can buy your book?"

"You don't have to buy my book, Vitor," I said, my inner fan-boy jumping up and down. "I'll give you a copy."

"You sign for me your name?"

"Yes, Vitor, I'd be more than happy to autograph it for you."

It was the best possible way to retire. In the crazy world of MMA, I will never be cooler than I was at that moment.

It was time to go home.

EPILOGUE
The Biggest Loser

"Deeds that do not involve risk bring no honor."

—PINDAR, ANCIENT GREEK POET

The last thing I wanted to do when I started this project was to start this project. But one of the best things I have ever done was to finish it. (Marrying Em, of course, is first on the list.) Over the previous decade, I had let myself go and I felt awkward, nasty, and bad about myself physically and emotionally. The rigors of MMA turned that around. When I began I was 250 pounds. Two years later, I fought at 185 pounds, and as of this writing my walking-around weight is 195. My blood pressure went from 145/100 to 118/80.

For nearly fifteen years, my Procrastination List was:

THINGS THAT MATT SHOULD DO STARTING TOMORROW BUT PROBABLY WON'T

1) Make money
2) Establish a writing career

3) Find a serious girlfriend
4) Marry her
5) Start a family
6) Get healthy
   a. Exercise more
   b. Eat smarter
   c. Drink less

I took nearly a decade of struggle and procrastinating to get my list down to this:

THINGS THAT MATT SHOULD DO STARTING TOMORROW BUT PROBABLY WON'T

1) ~~Make money~~
2) ~~Establish a writing career~~
3) ~~Find a serious girlfriend~~
4) Marry her
5) Start a family
6) Get healthy
   a. Exercise more
   b. Eat smarter
   c. Drink less

Once I started this project, it took only two years of MMA training before my list was reduced to this:

THINGS THAT MATT SHOULD DO STARTING TOMORROW BUT PROBABLY WON'T

1) ~~Make money~~
2) ~~Establish a writing career~~
3) ~~Find a serious girlfriend~~

4) ~~Marry her~~
5) Start a family
6) ~~Get healthy~~
   a. ~~Exercise more~~
   b. ~~Eat smarter~~
   c. ~~Drink less~~

Knock on wood, but I should live a longer and healthier life because of MMA. As mother pointed out, there are easier ways to lose weight and reduce one's blood pressure. But the easier ways are all easy to let slide and to procrastinate. I had done it for years. Nothing focuses the mind like unarmed combat. If it weren't for MMA, I'd still be the unhealthy, fat bastard I was before.

Mine is not an isolated example. I met dozens of men in their thirties and forties with similar stories. They had played sports in high school or college, but with the time demands of work and family had fallen into a physical rut. "I played football in college, but it's hard to get the time or a team together as you get older," one of the many guys I met told me in a typical personal story. "Three years ago I weighed 320 pounds. Then I took up MMA and I'm down to 230." Some savvy Fox TV executive should combine *The Ultimate Fighter* with *The Biggest Loser* and birth a fan-centric show. I'm open to negotiations for a hosting gig.

But deeper than physical fitness, there is a desire in students of MMA to find a sense of physical security. It seems odd that as a culture we spend so much time, money, and effort on teaching children how to throw, catch, and kick a ball. Fun games to be sure, but without much practical value. The Chinese have a saying: "The cultural and the martial are two halves of the whole." The idea was that the ideal person was educated both in the cultural classics and in the skills of fighting. After spending two years training in MMA, I feel a physical confidence that I had lost. MMA gave me back my swagger.

But beyond the personal self-improvement, I had a blast meeting all the various characters associated with the sport. It was a remarkable opportunity. What began as an assignment turned into passion. By and large, MMA fighters and trainers are some of the most open, quick-witted, and driven people I've ever met. Sure, a few were demented, but even they were my kind of crazy. They dream of being the best at something, and no matter how long the odds (there can be only one), no matter how great the pain, suffering, or sacrifice, they keep pursuing that dream day after day, hour after hour. One can debate whether they are the best athletes on the planet, but they are certainly the baddest.

And it was my great honor that for one night—even though everyone knew it was something of a lark and a publicity stunt— that I was treated, because I was willing like them to get into the ring, like a teammate.

AUTHOR'S NOTE

This book recounts the experiences of the author while he studied MMA for two years in New York, Bangkok, St. Petersburg, and Las Vegas as accurately as his aging, slightly punch-drunk brain would allow. A few names, however, were intentionally changed to protect the innocent. And as long as he is in a confessional mood, he would like to admit to an occasional reorganization of events for the sake of the narrative. He also wants to fess up to being far less charming and clever in real life than how he has portrayed himself in this book.

AUTHOR'S WIFE'S NOTE

I can confirm that the author is far less charming and clever in real life than how he portrayed himself in this book. Otherwise, the events recounted in this book are true. He really did abandon me for six months right after our wedding to live and train in Las Vegas. I should have married a novelist or one of those memoirists who makes everything up.

ACKNOWLEDGMENTS

"When drinking water, don't forget who dug the well."

—TRADITIONAL CHINESE PROVERB

First and foremost, I want to thank John Danaher, Phil Nurse, and Joey Varner, who shared not only their knowledge but also their lives with me. I hope this book does their generosity justice.

The fist connecting to my jaw on the front cover of this book belongs to my editor, Patrick Mulligan. That has made him—in the repressed, abused world of NYC publishing—a hero. Not only did he get to punch the face of an annoying, deadline-blowing author for five hours, but he got paid for the day to do it. Good for you, Patrick. Now it's my turn.

Special penance must go out to my publisher, Iron Bill Shinker—the hardest man in publishing. As my original eighteen-month contract was rewritten, and then extended, and then rewritten again, his patience for a passionate (i.e., lazy) writer was put to the test. Given the incredible list of authors he has published in his long and storied career, it is little surprise that he was a solid mixture of forgiveness and firmness. The book is infinitely better due to his mastery of when to give me some extra rope and when to take the manuscript from my cold, dead hands after I hanged myself.

"I realize I'm one of your slower writers," I said to my agent, Joe Veltre. To his great credit, he managed to exit his office before bursting into hysterical fits of laughter. Since I started this book, Joe has been hired by the Gersh Agency to run their book division. They are lucky to have him. And so am I.

With a project that spans two years of meeting amazing people, the most difficult part is deciding who has to be left out. Just to mention a few: Ron Frazier spent countless hours teaching me how to throw a proper left hook. Nik Fekete did the same for my sprawl. Jake Bonacci got me into the best shape of my life and prepared me for six minutes of fighting, despite my horrid eating habits. My training partner, Pat Begin, knew when to push me and was gracious enough to ease up when I couldn't keep up. Jacob "Stitch" Duran, the UFC's famous cutman, very generously sat for an extensive interview that helped me better understand what happens behind the scenes. I spent a wild Montreal weekend watching GSP fight Matt Serra with Ryan Harkness and Jacob Fortin at Fightlinker.com. It would make for a highly entertaining tale, if only we could remember what happened—*The Hangover Part III*.

But special thanks go to Robert Drysdale. I had an entire chapter devoted to him that ended up on the cutting room floor. He is one of the top grapplers in the world and a very positive coach. After every lesson I had with him, he would say things like "The good thing is that you listen to me, and that means you can improve." My jiu-jitsu improved greatly under his tutelage. Fortunately, I didn't need to test it in my fight, but if I had to, he was in my corner ready to guide me. And I can't thank him enough for that. All of the top MMA pros in Vegas train with Robert. If you are in Vegas and want to experience the best, pray he has an opening in his schedule.

A number of friends took time out of their busy schedules to review the manuscript for this book. Two in particular need to be thanked: Ryan Harkness (again) at Fightlinker.com and Ben Fowlkes at MMAFighting.com. Ryan suggested several hilarious off-color jokes. Ben deleted sections where I was coming off like an ungrateful snob who didn't appreciate the opportunity I was given. Also, as experts in the field, Ryan and Ben did their best to double-check my knowledge of MMA facts, figures, and history. In the process, they caught numerous errors. Of course, any remaining mistakes are entirely their fault. It's not like I didn't give them a chance to get it right in the first place. (So send your snarky, nitpicky emails to them, you trolls.)

Every time I start one of these projects, my father looks at me like "What did I do wrong?" But he very kindly keeps that to himself and is extremely supportive the entire way. And when it is done, he is as proud as he could be. The original Tiger Mother, Mama Polly always puts me back on the path of righteousness. When she read an early draft of this manuscript, she said, "Do you want my friends to think I raised a truck driver?" There are far fewer curse words in this book thanks to her Midwestern sense of propriety. You're the best, Mom.

When I was a single guy, I never really understood why married male writers were always praising their "angelic, patient" wives in the acknowledgments. The phrase struck me as slightly patronizing. After I started this project, I foolishly joked with Em: "We'll see how angelic and patient you turn out to be." That was before I abandoned her for six months to train in Vegas. Then the joke didn't seem so funny. One night I woke up to find her looking down at me. "You better refer to me as 'angelic and patient.'"

My sin, my soul, my summer rest, my heart, my brain, my everything, and all in between—you are as angelic as the choirs of heaven and as patient as Job. Can I stop sleeping on the couch now?